Davina Pardo

Bᴏʙ Mᴀɴᴋᴏғғ is the current cartoon editor for *The New Yorker* magazine. Before he succeeded Lee Lorenz as editor, Mankoff was a cartoonist for *The New Yorker* for twenty years. He founded the online Cartoon Bank, which has catalogued every cartoon since the magazine's founding. He is the author of the book *The Naked Cartoonist: A New Way to Enhance Your Creativity.*

ALSO BY BOB MANKOFF

The Naked Cartoonist: A New Way to Enhance Your Creativity

CARTOON COLLECTIONS

Elementary: The Cartoonist Did It

Urban Bumpkins

Call Your Office

It's Lonely at the Top

AS EDITOR

The Complete Cartoons of The New Yorker

On the Money: The Economy in Cartoons, 1925–2009

The New Yorker Caption Contest Book

The New Yorker Book of Literary Cartoons

The New Yorker Book of Business Cartoons

The New Yorker Book of Art Cartoons

The New Yorker Book of Teacher Cartoons

The New Yorker Book of Kids Cartoons

School Days: Cartoons from The New Yorker

HOW ABOUT NEVER

—

IS NEVER
GOOD FOR YOU?

HOW ABOUT NEVER
—
IS NEVER
GOOD FOR YOU?

MY LIFE IN CARTOONS

BOB MANKOFF

PICADOR

HENRY HOLT AND COMPANY

NEW YORK

picadorusa.com
twitter.com/picadorusa • facebook.com/picadorusa
picadorbookroom.tumblr.com

Picador® is a U.S. registered trademark and is used by Henry Holt and
Company under license from Pan Books Limited.

For book club information, please visit www.facebook.com/picadorbookclub or
e-mail marketing@picadorusa.com.

Designed by Toshiya Masuda

The Library of Congress has cataloged the Henry Holt edition as follows:

Mankoff, Robert.
    How about never—is never good for you? : my life in cartoons / Bob Mankoff. — First
edition.
        p. cm.
    ISBN 978-0-8050-9590-6 (hardcover)
    ISBN 978-0-8050-9591-3 (e-book)
    1. Mankoff, Robert.   2. Cartoonists—United States—Biography.   3. Periodical
editors—United States—Biography.   4. New Yorker (New York, N.Y. : 1925)   I. Title.
    NC1429.M358A2 2014
    741.5'6973—dc23
    [B]   2013021129

Picador Paperback ISBN 978-1-250-06242-0

Our books may be purchased in bulk for promotional, educational, or business use.
Please contact your local bookseller or the Macmillan Corporate and Premium
Sales Department at 1-800-221-7945, extension 5442, or by e-mail at
MacmillanSpecialMarkets@macmillan.com.

First published by Henry Holt and Company, LLC

First Picador Edition: October 2015

10   9   8   7   6   5   4

Dedicated to everyone who has ever done a cartoon for *The New Yorker*

Charles Addams, John Agee, Alain, Constantin Alajalov, Edward H. Allison, Gideon Amichay, C. W. Anderson, Geroge Annand, Robb Armstrong, Ed Arno, Peter Arno, Andrea Arroyo, Jose Arroyo, Jose Aruego, Niculae Asciu, Van Ass, T. K. Atherton, Aaron Bacall, Tom Bachtell, Peggy Bacon, Howard Baer, Bruce Bairnsfather, Ernest Hamlin Baker, Cyrus Baldridge, Perry Barlow, Bob Barnes, H. Barnes, Charles Barsotti, Donna Barstow, Ralph Barton, H. M. Bateman, Ross Bateup, Roland Baum, Glen Baxter, Ben Hur Baz, Alex Beam, Kate Beaton, Frank Beaven, Ludwig Bemelmans, Nora Benjamin, Bill Berg, Erik Bergstrom, Mike Berry, François Berthoud, Daniel Beyer, Michael Biddle, Reginald Birch, Kenneth Bird, Abe Birnbaum, Mahlon Blaine, Harry Bliss, Barry Blitt, A. Bloomberg, Victor Bobritsky, W. Bohanan, Ruben Bolling, Simon Bond, George Booth, David Borchart, Douglas Borgstedt, Irv. Breger, Herb Breneman, Wayne Bressler, Steve Brodner, Buck Brown, Chris Browne, M. K. Brown, Johan Bull, Gilbert Bundy, R. Van Buren, Loy Byrnes, Pat Byrnes, J. O. Cain, John Caldwell, E. Simms Campbell, Jerry Capa, D. T. Carlisle, Joe Carroll, H. H. Caviedes, Robert Censoni, Oscar Cesare, Tom Chalkley, P. Chapman, H. M. Charleton, Roz Chast, Tom Cheney, David Christianson, Robert Churchill, Richard Cline, Roger Clouse, Sam Cobean, Llyod Coe, Jonny Cohen, Mr. Colby, Nate Collier, Raul Colon, Russell Connor, J. S. Cook, John Corcoran, Jon Cornin, Frank Cotham, Miguel Covarrubias, Dave Coverly, Joseph Cowan, A. Cramer, Michael Crawford, Aline Kominsky-Crumb Robert Crumb, Leo Cullum, Andrej Czeczot, Gregory D'Alessio, D'Egville, C. Covert Darbyshire, Whitney Darrow Jr., Joe Dator, James Daugherty, Sal Davenport, Raymond Davidson, Baron Davis, Chon Day, Robert Day, Abner Dean, Richard Decker, Eldon Dedini, Paul Degen, Adolf Dehn, William de la Torre, Harold Denison, Victor de Pauw, Rodney de Sarro, Andre de Schaub, Drew Dernavich, Matthew Diffee, Rachel Domm, Liza Donnelly, John Donohue, Leonard Dove, Nick Downes, Eric Drooker, Boris Drucker, John Drummond, Steve Duenes, J. C. Duffy, Gerald Dumas, Alan Dunn, Roger Duvoisin, Caroline Dworin, William Dwyer, E. K. Easton, Bob Eckstein, Isaac Littlejohn Eddy, K. R. Edwards, E. J. Ellison, John Elmore, W. J. Enright, Benita Epstein, Carl Eric Ericson, Alden Erikson, Rob Esmay, Jaro Fabry, Graham Falk, Joseph Fannel, Joseph Farris, Nancy Fay, Jules Feiffer, Rich Feldmann, Alan Ferguson, Michael Ffolkes, Liana Finck, Ed Fisher, Emily Flake, Floherty Jr., Douglas Florian, Corey Ford, Evan Forsch, Alan Foster, Dana Fradon, Anthony Fraioli, Arnoldo Franchioni, Andre Francois, Edward Frascino, Ian Frazier, Margaret Freeman, Alberto Fremura, Drew Friedman, K. Friedrick, Alfred Frueh, Tom Funk , Roger Furse, J. H. Fyfe, William Crawford Galbraith, D. W. Gale, Felipe Galindo, Robert Gallivan, P. G. Garetto, Eli Garson, M. Gauerke, Arthur Geisert, Thurston Gentry, Mort Gerberg, Arthur Getz, Mary Gibson, Mimi Gnoli, Herbert Goldberg, Walter Goldstein, Douglas Gordon, Edward Gorey, Bud Grace, Martha Gradisher, A. S. Graham, Edward Graham, Greasley, Gerald Green, William Green, Alex Gregory, William Gropper, Milton Gross, Sam Gross, Robert Grossman, John Groth, Tom Hachtman, William Haefeli, Harry W. Haenigsen, Kaamran Hafeez, William Hamilton, Malcom Hancock, J. B. Handelsman, Frank Hanely, Charlie Hankin, Sidney Harris, Alice Harvey, William Heaslip, Piet Hein, W. E. Heitland, John Held Jr., O. Herford, Justin Herman, Don Herold, Leo Hershfield, Eric Hilgerdt, Ned Hilton, Trevor Hoey, Sydney Hoff, H. O. Hofman, Helen E. Hokinson, Tom Holloway, Bernard Hollowood, Pete Holmes, Ellison Hoover, Marshall Hopkins, Oscar Howard, E. F. Hubbard, Albert Hubbell, D. Huffine, Stan Hunt, Phil Hustis, Amy Hwang, E. F. Hynes, Benoît van Innis, Rea Irvin, David Jacobson, Louis Jamme, Sewell Johnson, John Jonik, Maira Kalman, Kamagurka, John Kane, Zachary Kanin, Bruce Eric Kaplan, Paul Karasik, Nurit Karlin, Farley Katz, Al Kaufman, Jeff Kaufman, John Kaunus, Jeff Keate, Yann Kebbi, Robert Keith, Eldon Kelley, Jim Kelly, T. E. Kennedy, Gilbert Kerlin, John Kerschbaum, Hank Ketchum, Ted Key, Ham Khan, Roch King, David L. Kingman, Rollin Kirby, James E. Kirchman, Tom Kleh, I. Klein, John Klossner, Clayton Knight, H. H. Knight, Bob Knox, Leo Kober, Edward Koren, Anatol Kovarsky, Fernando Krahn, Krakusin, Robert Kraus, John Kreuttner, Ken Krimstein, Peter Kuper, Ralph Lane, David Langdon, Lapcheck, Carol Lay, John Leavitt, Frederico LeBrun, Bill Lee, Stuart Leeds, Alfred Leete, Robert Leighton, Glen LeLievre, Robert Lennen, Monroe Leung, Arnie Levin, David Levine, Eric Lewis, Glen Le Lievre, Peter Lippman, Hendrik W. Van Loon, Lee Lorenz, Robert Love, Cliff C. Lozell, Mike Luckovich, Fred Lundy, Roberta Macdonald, A. Edwin Macon, Steve Macone, Gus Mager, Kenneth Mahood, Henry Major, Hancock Malcom, Christina Malman, Robert Malone, Robert Mankoff, Marisa Acocella Marchetto, Jerry Marcus, Jack Markow, Reginald Marsh, Huguette Martel, Charles E. Martin, Michael Maslin, R. J. Matson, Rip Matteson, Doris Matthews, Bill Mauldin, Ernest Maxwell, Bruce McCall, Richard McCallister, Ann McCarthy, F. McIntosh, William

McIntyre, Dorothy McKay, Donald McKee, E. McNerney, Taggart C. McVicker, Sam Means, Jack Medoff, Roland Michaud, Mario Micossi, Eugène Mihaesco, Warren Miller, John Milligan, Robert Minter, Joseph Mirachi, Julian de Miskey, Frank Modell, Ariel Molvig, Guy Montone, Wallace Morgan, Jack Moscowitz , Robert Muccio, Peter Mueller, James Mulligan, Lou Myers, Merle Nacht, Ruth Nash, Fred Neher, Ralph Newman, Louis Nitka, Ed Nofziger, Alphonse Normandia, John Norment, Paul Noth, William O'Brian, John O'Brien, Mark O'Donnell, C. E. O'Glass, Sean O'Neill, Richard Oldden, George Olden, Pat Oliphant, Everett Opie, Robert Orr Palmer, Kathy Osborn, Corey Pandolph, Gary Panter, Robert Paplow, W. B. Park, Virgil F. Partch, David Pascal, Jason Patterson, Victor De Pauw, Ralph E. Pearson, Augustus Peck, Ralph Pekor, M. K. Perker, C. F. Peters, Bruce Petty, Mary Petty, Rini Piccolo, Ethel Plummer, Jason Polan, Peter Porges, George Price, Garrett Price, John M. Price, Louis Priscilla, Lee Purcell, Pusey, Radford, Michael Rae-Grant, Gardner Rea, Lillian Reed, John Reehill, Paul Reilly, Harry Rein, Doug Reina, John Reynolds, Gaspano Ricca, Emily Richards, Mischa Richter, William Von Riegen, Donald Reilly, George Riemann, J. P. Rini, Robert Risko, Riveron, Cliff Roberts, Victoria Roberts, Boardman Robinson, W. Heath Robinson, Charles Rodrigues, Dean Rohrer, Stephen Ronay, Carl Rose, Al Ross, Herb Roth, John Ruge, Douglas Ryan, William Sakren, Rodney de Sarro, Charles Sauers, Jennifer Saura, Brian Savage, Charles Saxon, August J. Schallack, Schaub, Jim Schmalzried, Walter Schmidt, Howard Schneider, Bernard Schoenbaum, Adolf Schus, Benjamin Schwartz, William Scully, Ronald Searle, J. J. Sempe, Neil Sessa, Seth, Burr Shafer, Danny Shanahan, George V. Shanks, Michael Shaw, George Shellhase, Barbara Shermund, Vahan Shirvanian, E. L. Shoemaker, Bud Van Sickle, Dink Siegel, L. H. Siggs, R. Sikoryak, Andrew Singer, David Sipress, Stephanie Skalisky, Barbara Smaller, Francis Smilby, Claude Smith, F. E. Smith, J. K. Smith, Henry Holmes Smith, Ton Smits, Karen Sneider, David Snell, Otto Soglow, Aaron Sopher, Edward Sorel, Leo Soretsky, M. Van Sort, Art Spiegelman, Mark Alan Stamaty, J. Stanley, Leslie Starke, Kemp Starrett, Edward Steed, William Steig, Henry Anton Steig, David Stein, Avi Steinberg, Saul Steinberg, Peter Steiner, Hans Stengel, Mick Stevens, James Stevenson, Jack Stockwell, Storm, Susanne Suba, Ed Subitsky, A. M. Suggs, Julia Suits, Ward Sutton, Anthony Taber, Richard Taylor, Eric Teitelbaum, R. Thayer, Mark Thompson, C. Throckmorton, James Thurber, Tidden, Jack Tippet, Barney Tobey, Tom Tomorrow, Tom Toro, William de la Torre, Tousey, Irwin Touster, M. Towle, S. Trachtenberg, W. P. Trent, Larry Trepel, Charles Tudor, Buford Tune, Mike Twohy, Ed Umansky, Eben A. Valentine, R. Van Buren, Hendrik Van Loon, Bud Van Sickle, M. Van Sort, P. C. Vey, Dean Vietor, S. Wade, T. Waldeyer, John S. P. Walker, Liam Walsh, Dearing Ward, Eric Monroe Ward, Kim Warp, Noel Watson, Arthur Watts, Steve Way, Paul Webb, Robert Weber, Philippe Weisbecker, Andrew Weldon, Christopher Weyant, Shannon Wheeler, Wiggins, A. F. Wiles, Fred Wilkinson, Gilbert Wilkinson, Gluyas Williams, Herb Williams, Wilton Williams, Gahan Wilson, George Wilson, Bernie Wiseman, Horace Wofford, W. Wolfson, Lawson Wood, Bill Woodman, Denys Wortman, G. Wright, Richard Yardley, Art Young, Bertrand Zadig, Roz Zanengo, A. Zeiger, Jack Ziegler

AND TO ANYONE WHO EVER WILL.

Hopefuls, write your name below and maybe in subsequent printings of this book it will appear above.

_____, _____, _____, _____, _____,
_____, _____, _____, _____, _____,
_____, _____, _____, _____, _____,
_____, _____, _____, _____, _____,
_____, _____, _____, _____, _____,
_____, _____, _____, _____, _____,
_____, _____, _____, _____, _____,
_____, _____, _____, _____, _____,
_____, _____, _____, _____, _____,
_____, _____, _____, _____, _____,
_____, _____, _____, _____, _____,
_____, _____, _____, _____, _____,
_____, _____, _____, _____, _____,
_____, _____, _____, _____, _____,
_____, _____, _____, _____, _____,
_____, _____, _____, _____, _____,
_____, _____, _____, _____, _____,
_____, _____, _____, _____, to be continued

CONTENTS

HOW ABOUT NEVER
—
IS NEVER
GOOD FOR YOU?

R. Mankoff
WELCOME

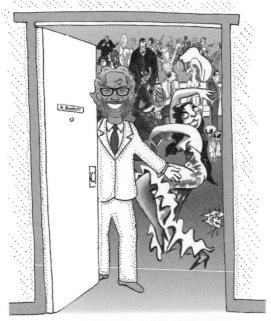

INTRODUCTION

*S*ince this is an introduction, I think it only appropriate that I introduce myself.

Hi, I'm Bob Mankoff, cartoon editor of *The New Yorker* magazine. I may not have the best job in the world, but I'm in the running.

Actually, I have the best *jobs* in the world. For my day job, I get to see more than five hundred cartoons every week from the best cartoonists. I also moonlight as a cartoonist for *The New Yorker* and have contributed more than nine hundred cartoons myself. The caption of my most famous one is now so firmly entrenched in the culture as an all-purpose put-down phrase that it can be referenced as though it were an anonymous aphorism; Nancy Pelosi did just that during the 2012 election.

Probably just a coincidence that the marketing mavens behind this book chose it as the title.

Okay, now you have me at a disadvantage. You know a little something about me, but I know zip about you, except for one thing: you like *New Yorker* cartoons. Why else would you be reading this?

Well, that makes two of us, and unless those same marketing mavens are very much mistaken, there are quite a few more likers like us. There better be. I'm sure you're a swell person and I'm not a bad guy myself, but publishing a book for just the two of us wouldn't make much sense.

And as much as we both like *New Yorker* cartoons, it wouldn't make sense for this book to just be another collection of *New Yorker* cartoons. There are plenty of those. Hey, I should know.

The New Yorker Book of Teacher Cartoons
> Robert Mankoff
★★★★☆ (14)

The New Yorker Book of Kids Cartoons
> Robert Mankoff
★★★★☆ (3)

The New Yorker Book of Literary Cartoons
Bob Mankoff
★★★★★ (4)

School Days: Cartoons from the New Yorker
> Robert Mankoff
★★★☆☆ (2)

So, what exactly is this book about? Long story short, me. Look, it's a memoir, and you can't spell memoir without the *moi*. But short story a little longer, it's summed up nicely in the contract I signed to do the book.

> **THE WORK, THE GRANT OF RIGHTS, TERRITORY AND DURATION**
> I. (a) This Agreement concerns a work provisionally entitled **HOW ABOUT NEVER...IS NEVER GOOD FOR YOU?** to be written and illustrated by **Robert Mankoff** which will be a work of nonfiction, approximately forty thousand (40,000) words in length, which will be a memoir in words, cartoons, and assorted imagery encompassing the Author's childhood and career as a cartoonist and the art and psychology of humor, including anecdotes from fifteen years as cartoon editor of *The New Yorker* and loaded with more than one hundred cartoons spanning the Author's thirty year career (the "Work").

That pretty much lays it out and doesn't do too bad a job, although it does underestimate the number of cartoons by a factor of three. And as contracts are not meant to be funny, it isn't. But this book is, and not just because of the cartoons.

I feel if something is worth saying, it's worth saying funny. That's why even though the contract specified forty thousand words, I ended up with only thirty-six thousand, because the other ones weren't funny enough.

But all the laughs have a narrative purpose: to tell my story as a person, cartoonist, and cartoon editor within the larger story of the extraordinary institution that made magazine cartooning an important part of American culture, *The New Yorker*. So, I'm going to, as it were, show the soup-to-nuts process of cartoon creation, selection, editing, and publishing that makes a *New Yorker* cartoon unique and delectable. Along the way, you'll get to know not only me but also the fascinating cast of cartoonists and editors who make all of this possible. And for the icing on the cake, I'm going to tell you how to win our famous caption contest.

Even though this book is relatively short, I've been working on it for a long time—really, my whole life as a cartoonist and cartoon editor. At least in the back of my mind I have. But a number of things precipitated moving it to the front.

First was my reinvolvement, after a thirty-year absence, in academic psychology. In the 1970s, I was an all-but-PhD student when I quit to become a cartoonist. Some thirty years later, I discovered that the field I'd abandoned could help me better understand the field I was in, and vice versa. In my absence, an entire discipline devoted to the study of humor had sprung up.

Putting all my all-but-PhD expertise to good use, I've been using cartoons to do research into humor and then using that research to better understand cartoons. One of the things I've learned along the way is that although humor is a fascinating topic, academics, being academics, can take the fun out of it and make it boring. Not to worry—I'm not a real academic.

However, I won't be constantly "on." That would be as tedious as being always "off." Besides, much as I hate to admit it, you can't explain everything with a joke, especially another joke. That would lead to an "infinite regression," in which each joke would have to be explained by another joke, eventually using up all the jokes in the world and leaving us with a very sad planet with one damn joke still to be explained.

Still, there's a middle ground, a sweet spot for the use of humor in explaining humor, and cartoons are often the spot-on way to hit it.

"Too soon?"

So, fearlessly, but hopefully not foolishly, I've ignored E. B. White's famous admonition that "analyzing humor is like dissecting a frog. Few people are interested and the frog dies of it." In fact, my online *New Yorker* newsletter is all about this analysis.

And even though the occasional frog bites the dust, no mass amphibian extinction occurs.

"We will always have Paris."

The second thing that prompted me to actually put pen to paper was that writing the newsletter every week let me develop a writing style that was truly my own, using images and text in an organic way (the way I'm doing here) in which each reinforced the other. Technology now allowed me to access an illustrative cartoon as quickly as an app might autocorrect a word.

"Oh, I see what happened. Autocorrect changed 'southpaw' to 'sauerkraut.'"

The third motivating factor was the realization that I wasn't going to be the cartoon editor of *The New Yorker* forever—not because I plan to retire anytime soon, but because I'm not going be anything forever, including, alas, sob, alive.

I mean, I'm relatively young if you consider sixty-nine to be relatively young, which I don't, but relatively soon I'll be pushing seventy from the wrong side. This cartoon notwithstanding,

"Good news, honey—seventy is the new fifty."

I figured it might be a good idea to do my memoiring while I still had plenty of memory to memoir with.

Fourthly and finally, while the nature of memoiring is to look back, I realized that I had a lot to look forward to. And you, *New Yorker* cartoon liker, do too, because after fifteen years, my main goal upon becoming cartoon editor had been achieved.

When I took over as cartoon editor, in 1997, I inherited a great bunch of cartoonists. Many of their cartoon characters are behind me in the opening image of this introduction. And many of them are still doing great cartoons for us. Only, if I couldn't help develop a new generation on my watch, eventually, alas, sob, there would be no more *New Yorker* cartoons. But stay your tears, because that new generation is here in force, and as a force it is changing the nature of what it means to be a *New Yorker* cartoon.

Still, with all due immodesty, they wouldn't be here without me, so before getting to their story, I think I should tell mine. The only question is when to start. How about now—is now good for you?

I'M NOT ARGUING, I'M JEWISH

People often ask me about my upbringing, and if there was anything particular about it that made me become a cartoonist.

To that, I could reply, "If you really want to hear about it, the first thing you'll probably want to know is where I was born, and what my lousy childhood was like, and how my parents were occupied and all before they had me, and all that David Copperfield kind of crap, but I don't feel like going into it, if you want to know the truth."

But I don't, because if you want to know the truth, that is the first paragraph of J. D. Salinger's *The Catcher in the Rye* and has nothing to do with me—except that I first read that book back in my eleventh-grade English class and have been hoping ever since that I could work it into something I was writing, and now I have. So let me throw in a Salinger *New Yorker* cartoon of mine for good measure.

"And, in literary news, J.D. Salinger's privacy has been violated once again by his appearance in this cartoon."

But enough about Salinger. He's dead now, and I'm still hanging in there.

So, let's move back to the influences of my un-lousy childhood, in which I was the much loved (maybe too much loved) and doted upon only child of Lou and Mollie Mankoff, here seen in 1939, the year they were married.

No doubt I was doted on somewhat for my eminent dotableness.

Mollie was flamboyant and needy. Lou was reserved and giving. It was a case of the reserved Lou finding in the emotional Mollie someone who could complete him, and of Mollie finding someone who could balance her emotionalism. Besides, Mollie was hot. There's an old song that goes,

Whatever Lola wants
Lola gets.

Substitute "Mollie" for "Lola" and you have the idea.

Anyway, Lou gave.

A song popular in 1943 had the lyrics "Just Molly and me / And baby makes three / we're happy in my blue heaven." And by 1944 Mollie and Lou did have me, not in my blue heaven but the Bronx. Actually, when I was born it was really Mollie and me, with no Lou around, because he was away doing his bit in the Big One, while Mollie doted on the little one back home.

"Doting" is probably too mild a word to describe my mother's obsessive attention to my existence, so long in doubt (there had been a number of miscarriages) and which she felt could be snatched away from her at any time. I'm told that when I was sleeping, she would put a mirror up to my mouth to see if it would fog over, showing that I was indeed breathing and alive. I still do that myself, every once in a while, just to make sure. I think Mollie's ministrations instilled in me a potential for hypochondria, a potential that has been fully realized and has made its way into a number of my cartoons, with the name used in them no coincidence.

"Well, Bob, it looks like a paper cut, but just to be sure let's do lots of tests."

"Nothing serious, Bob—just a case of the forties."

Or maybe I just inherited the disposition from her. She was what I would call in robust ill health her whole long life (she lived to ninety-three). Whenever I asked her how she felt, she would always reply, "Not a hundred percent." I think her high-water mark was around seventy-four percent. Whether about a real or imagined illness or some other problem, real or imagined, my mother was either panicking or making preparations to panic, and my father was always there ready to say, "This too shall pass" and stick with it until whatever was troubling Mollie did pass.

During the war, my father had to placate my mother from afar by mail. In one letter, he tries to calm her by explaining that it's not a lack of love that's causing the lack of letters she's getting from him but army logistics.

A lot of what you need to know about my dad is in that letter. Even as he complains about her complaining, he says, "I know how you feel and can hardly blame you . . . everybody likes to get mail." He also had a dry sense of humor. In another letter he mentions a handbag he has sent her and quips, "It's pretty popular in Paris, so it should be OK in the Bronx."

And despite the war and wartime postal problems, things were okay in the Bronx, if a bit crowded. In addition to my mom, there were my mom's mother and father, my mom's sisters, Annie and Sarah, Sarah's husband, Jack, and their kids, my cousins, Mike, Joan, and Irwin, all crammed into the top floor of a little house at 1453 Teller Avenue.

In 1945 my dad came home from the war. He was a welcome sight to my mother and everyone else in the household, except me. I had never laid eyes on him, or vice versa. My mother had gotten pregnant while he was on leave, and he'd been sent overseas a few months before I was born. Family lore has it that when I saw him for the first time, I cried, "Who is that man!"

That man, and the rest of us, confronted a severe postwar housing shortage in New York at that time, which this contemporaneous *New Yorker* cartoon refers to:

This led to the landlord of 1453 needing the top floor (where we all lived) for his own relatives, which led to us, all of us, being booted out, all the way to Queens. Ex-sergeant Lou Mankoff took command, marching his troops from B (the Bronx) to Q (Queens).

There, all of us decamped to a little house not all that different from the previous one, but now we occupied both floors. Luxury.

Two years later, my dad used a VA loan to buy the house right next door, and me, my dad, my mom, and my aunt Anne moved there: 76-37 169th Street, just the four of us, with two floors all our own—the lap of luxury.

Really. And the lap was about to get larger. The booming fat fifties of postwar America were just around the corner, with television, air-conditioning, and a new car in the garage every two years (if it could fit).

Not to mention wall-to-wall carpeting, which I really have to mention because this particular postwar luxury was the way my dad earned a living. He was the owner of Atlas Floors, selling wall-to-wall carpeting, a previously out-of-reach luxury that was available, for the first time, to a middle class now flush with some surplus cash. Wall-to-wall in the new living room said you'd arrived and were a stakeholder in the American dream. Due to wall-to-wall, we were soon living that dream.

"I had the most marvellous dream last night. The whole world was done over in wall-to-wall carpeting."

Lou was, as they used to say, a good provider, pulling down fifty thousand dollars a year by the end of the decade, when a slice of pizza and *The New Yorker* both cost only fifteen cents. But the providing didn't come easy. He left for his store before seven A.M. and didn't return home until late at night. Sunday was the only day he ever took off, and, exhausted, he always slept past noon that day. The upshot was that he wasn't the constant, mirror-up-to-the-mouth (at least metaphorically) presence in my life that my mother was. That, combined with the fact that for nearly the first two years of my life he'd been absent, amplified the effect of my mother's presence on me.

And, *oy gevalt*, what a presence: an old-school, you shouldn't know from it, but nevertheless now you're knowing from it, Jewish mother's presence.

Oy gevalt is Yiddish, loosely translated into English as "Oh goodness," but you really can't easily translate Yiddish into English without losing something important—its humor. "*Oy gevalt!*" is funny; "Oh goodness" isn't. *Mishegas, bupkes, kvetch* are funny; their English equivalents—"craziness," "nothing," and "complain"—aren't. And words like *schlemiel* and *schlimazel* are funny not just because of how they sound but because they are best defined through a joke: a *schlemiel* (bungler) is someone who spills his soup on a *schlimazel* (unfortunate person).

My mother spoke fluent Yiddish. As I was growing up, she would variously call me a *klainer hunt* ("little dog"), a *groisser ferd* ("big horse"), and, when I was particularly annoying, a *narvez choleryeh* ("nervous plague"—literally, cholera). All of those terms, both endearing and insulting, are the kind of two-faced communication Yiddish excels at, combining aggression, friendliness, and ambiguity, a basic recipe for humor that my mother was excellent at cooking up and on which I was spoon-fed.

But even when she wasn't sprinkling her English with Yiddishisms, the humorous influence of Yiddish was there.

If I told her I didn't like a certain food I had never complained about before—like the egg salad sandwiches she made every damn day for my school lunch—she would say, "Since when did you throw a hate on egg salad?" If I said I was bored, she would answer, "You're bored? So go knock your head against the wall, you won't be bored." And if I answered her back, "Which wall?" I'd get back "Would you look at the mouth on him." Right, Mom—your mouth.

What she said, I gainsaid. Or as she would put it, "If I say black, you say blue." I added my own funny spin to everything, using material from the wider culture for our exchanges. Once when she complained to my father that I was lazy, saying, "Lou, he don't do nothin'," I shot back,

"He don' plant taters, he don't plant cotton
An' dem dat plants 'em is soon forgotten."

She wouldn't have laughed at that. My mother wasn't logical or knowledgeable. What she was, was intuitive. She wasn't really an audience for my jokes, she was a target. And, as my therapist would tell you, still is. Yet I've gotten a lot from her, including a mother lode of material, some of which I'm unloading here. Although my relationship with my mother was less than ideal from a relationship standpoint, from a development-of-humor standpoint it worked very well. Humor thrives on conflict

and needs a target.

She was the first.

Others came later, like the kids on "the block"—all my Jewish boyhood friends: Larry Kantor, Danny Kleiman, Stevie Roth, Ricky Werber. We fought all the time. Not with our fists—punching is not my tribe's preferred technique. We preferred insults, in endless hours of arguing and ranking out and putting down, none of which would be worthy of the Algonquin Round Table and wouldn't even have made the grade here:

THE CELEBRATED WITS OF THE RADISSON ROUND TABLE.

But the important thing for me in all this jousting was that I put the "mouth I had on me" to good use, giving better than I got, and training my brain to be on the lookout for anything in any interaction that had worthy comic potential.

So, how did all this rub off on me? When I was first dating my wife, Cory, who is not Jewish, we once were having what I thought was an ordinary conversation, and she said, "Why are you arguing with me?" I replied, "I'm not arguing, I'm Jewish." Which means, to me, the questioning of everything just for the hell of it and then questioning the questioning just for the fun of it and the funny in it. The expression "Two Jews, three opinions" sums it up nicely and funnily.

Jews are overthinkers. It's no surprise that we invented psychoanalysis. Humor is the antidote to overthinking. It's a way of saying that life is paradoxical. Humor contains contradictions; it does not resolve them but revels in them. It says that the right way to exist among the contradictions, paradoxes, and absurdities of life is to cope with them through laughter.

Now, I don't want to overdo this Jewish thing. On the other hand, I don't want to underdo it, either. A study done in 1978 showed that although Jews constituted only 3 percent of the U.S. population, 80 percent of the nation's comedians, at that time, were Jewish.

The first generation of Jewish comics grew up in large Yiddish-speaking immigrant families and anglicized their names. So Benjamin Kubelsky became

Jack Benny, Nathan Birnbaum was reborn as

George Burns, and Milton Berlinger—well, you can figure that one out.

And even though they had changed their names and the general public didn't identify them as Jewish, *we* knew. It didn't involve any telltale mannerisms or Yiddish words. Whenever any of them would appear on TV my mother would say, "You know, he's Jewish."

Everyone knew that the second generation of Jewish comics—men like Lenny Bruce (Leonard Schneider), Jerry Lewis (Joseph Levitch), Mel Brooks (Melvin Kaminsky), and Woody Allen (Allan Konigsberg)—were Jewish, but by changing their names they followed an old saying: "Think Yiddish but dress British."

Interestingly, when I was an adolescent my mother suggested that I could get a nose job if I wanted and, when the time came, change my name to Robert Mann. Back then, to be really good-looking and really Jewish-looking was an oxymoron. But while this advice from your mother might be damaging to your psyche and result in many years in analysis,

it also created a psychodynamic conflict of feeling both superior intellectually and inferior physically, causing a tension that humor was better at relieving than a nose job, or at least less expensive.

"Too Jewish?"

By the way, that 1978 study I mentioned also pointed out something else of relevance to me. It said that, in general, these comedians had overprotective, constrictive mothers and a drive to break out of the Jewish world and gain general acceptance. I'm sure that's an overgeneralization, but I'm also sure that it nails things in my case, certainly as regards my mother. As for the part about breaking out from the Jewish world and seeking wider acclaim, I think the seeds of that were planted, ironically enough, at my big fat 1950s bar mitzvah celebration at the Hotel Pierre, in 1957.

My imagination was really stirred that night by the guy on the right, who scooted around the stage, singing, dancing, and tummling: Nat Brooks, the fearless, funny leader of the Nat Brooks Orchestra.

Nat was hip, cool, definitely meshuga, and, despite the anglicized last name, clearly Jewish. I remember him playing the piano from under the piano, backward.

He also parodied different genres, used props, and infused all the music with a comic flavor.

Nat was a talented musician. In fact, he was a classically trained pianist. As talented as he was in that field, however, on musical talent alone he wouldn't have carved out the niche he did for himself, if he hadn't combined it with humor. And his comedic talent, even though good, would not have been good enough for him to be a stand-alone comedian. But, like they say (and I'm glad they're saying it rather than me, because it's such a hackneyed cliché), "the sum was greater than the total of the parts." I also would need an analogous combination of my humor and some other talent to avoid going the usual route, in which you make your Jewish parents proud by becoming (in descending order of the joyful kvelling associated with the profession) a doctor, lawyer, dentist, or accountant.

Spoiler alert: That other talent is going to be art. But before we go there, a brief digression on Jerry Lewis and his influence on me.

During the 1950s, my parents often took me to the Catskills on vacation. We'd stay at Brown's Hotel, the place made famous by Jerry Lewis, who got his start there and later played to crowds in its Jerry Lewis Playhouse. The roads on the way to the Catskills were full of billboards for Brown's, with a gigantic head of Jerry Lewis

sticking up above the sign; underneath, large letters announced, "Jerry Lewis says Brown's is my favorite resort."

Here I am with my family at Brown's in 1958:

In skinny, goofy, manic Jerry Lewis I could see something of my own skinny, goofy, manic self. First of all, there's a physical resemblance. His caricature on that billboard would have worked pretty well for an adolescent me:

And it's not hard to imagine the nine-year-old me, on the left, growing up to look like him:

It was much more natural for me to identify with Lewis than with Jack Benny or George Burns. Stylistically, the wacky, googly-eyed slapstick of something like *The Nutty Professor*

was a lot easier to emulate than the perfectly timed one-liners of George Burns or the carefully calibrated double takes of Jack Benny. Jerry had a big mouth, literally, and could do this:

So could I (you'll have to take my word for it). Not very classy, but being a class clown doesn't involve class. Also, as outrageous, silly, and childish as doing that is, there is something to be said for it. That's why I'm saying it. Acting outrageously makes it that much easier to think unconventionally. If you don't have a silly bone in your body, you're not going to have a funny bone, either. And if you can't combine a mature intelligence with some immature thinking, you're never going to be funny enough to make a living at it.

So, given all this, why didn't I set my sights on being the next Jerry Lewis? Well, I could say—and I think everyone would agree, with the possible exception of the French—that one Jerry Lewis is enough. But the truth is, I had no ambition to be Jerry Lewis, because I had no ambition at all. I was just a kid happy to do what I liked and be liked for doing what I liked, whether it was clowning around or drawing. We've covered the clowning, so now let's move on to the drawing.

CHAPTER TWO

WE'RE LOOKING FOR PEOPLE WHO LIKE TO DRAW

There were lots of ads like this one in magazines when I was growing up. Look, the almost naked lady in that ad might have been the thing that caught my eye, but I was more fascinated by the idea that drawing pictures was something you could do as an adult. And even if you weren't drawing almost naked ladies, it still seemed like a good job, because it wasn't a job at all, and what kid wants a job? Not me. I just liked to draw; I drew all the time. It was fun. Here's a dour, un-fun guy I call "the Russian," who I drew when I was about seven.

More frequently, I copied characters like Bugs Bunny and Donald Duck out of comic books.

As you can see, my talent in drawing them was no great shakes. A parent might kvell over these sketches, but that was about it. On the other hand, if you added the secret sauce of humor, attention would be paid, and in the coin of the comic realm: laughter. The sauce could be with words

Ehh, what's up, Duck?

or visual:

Simple stuff, but it does perhaps foreshadow the mashing up of ideas from different frames of reference that I would use many times over in creating somewhat more sophisticated *New Yorker* cartoons like these:

MILITARY SOLUTION TO LAST WEEK'S PUZZLE

"Say what's on your mind, Harris—the
language of dance has always eluded me."

Still, my parents weren't suggesting that I quit school to pursue a career in cartooning. I wasn't suggesting it, either.

Time passed—a lot of time—and things changed—a lot of things—and some years ago, at my daughter's high school, I gave a Career Day talk about my thirty-five-year "career" in cartooning. I do these talks in the hope that I can prevent one young person, especially if they are Jewish, from becoming a doctor, lawyer, dentist, or accountant. On these occasions I always ask if anyone wants to become a cartoonist. If I get any positive response I say, "That's great. You can quit school right now." I always hasten to add—as I'm being summarily escorted out of the building—that this is only a joke and you should not quit school, because if you do, you won't be able to make fun of a better class of things, such as Shakespeare,

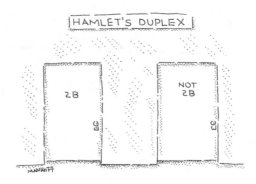

economics,

"Bad news on Wall Street today, as the bottom fell out of the market, the sides collapsed, and the top blew away."

or even Judaism.

"And remember, if you need anything I'm available 24/6."

Anyway, I stayed in school, and by the time I was ready for high school, my drawing ability had improved from the gloomy Russian guy to this portrait inspired by a newspaper photograph:

Even though it seems to be missing an ear, it was good enough to cause my art teacher in Junior High School 216 to suggest that I compile a portfolio of my drawings and apply to the High School of Music and Art. It really should have been called Music *or* Art, because students did one or the other but not both. Which was good for me, because while I could draw a wheelbarrow, I couldn't carry a tune in one. Years later, Music and Art merged with the High School of Performing Arts. A fictionalized version of that school became the basis for the movie *Fame*.

I didn't attain any fame at Music and Art. However, careful study of anatomy taught me that the human head has two ears and eventually earned me this diploma:

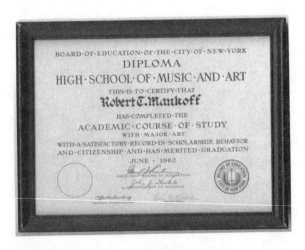

Despite what my diploma claims, I don't think my teachers at M&A would have said that my behavior was "satisfactory." "Satiric" would be more like it. Whenever the teacher wasn't looking, I would draw cartoons mocking what was going on in class. Every once in a while a teacher would wheel around and catch me at it, saying something like "Robert, if you think that's so funny, perhaps you would like to share it with the rest of the class!" And I'd always reply, "Indeed I would." But it was always the principal I ended up sharing with.

While Music and Art didn't offer a course in satire, the arts program had courses in figure drawing, painting, architecture, and sculpture.

I still have this work of mine from a bygone sculpture class:

I've taken to calling him Quasimodo, but the piece was actually inspired by this image of Rocky Marciano knocking out Jersey Joe Walcott:

What the sculpture lacks in anatomical accuracy (clearly I was still having some problems in the depiction of ears) I think it makes up for in emotional intensity. Still, most of my emotional intensity in that class was directed toward Alice Garin, seen in her mug shot from our 1962 yearbook:

Alice Garin

Nice mug, but weird hairdo. I think it was inspired by the early '60s pillbox hat craze.

I really had a case of the hots for Alice, who, unfortunately, had a case of the cools for me. But spurned ardor is not necessarily diminished ardor, and I can still recall many a fantasy she inspired.

I eventually sublimated my unrequited lust for Alice and redirected my erotic energy not to art but to basketball. M&A, which was located in what is called Spanish Harlem, had a basketball team and, in fact, competed against some pretty tough inner-city schools. I tried out for it every year and finally, harnessing all my repressed libidinal energy, made the team during my senior year.

Can you pick me out? Hint: I didn't used to be black, Hispanic, or blond, am wearing a T-shirt to hide the enormously overdeveloped musculature in my arms, and look more like Jerry Lewis than anyone else in the photo.

Our team was surprisingly good that year, considering the league we played in and how much the other teams reviled us. The prospect of losing to artsy-fartsy Music and Artsy was really humiliating for these macho schools. And from our perspective, it was hard to sink a shot while constantly being taunted by cries of "Shoot the ball, faggot." How to respond? Well, in addition to my signature offensive move of appearing to throw up and then suddenly shooting, I also employed my signature humor by replying to the faggot taunts with "I will as soon as my nails dry."

I'm most proud of the innovative defensive maneuver I developed in an intraleague game against the Bronx High School of Science, the one school that could outnerd us. Here I am employing it against some elongated geek who is calculating the parabolic arc of his shot, which he is never going to hit because I'm about to snatch his glasses away.

Despite innovations like this one, I was not the star of the team. That would be Fred Thaler, three to my left in the team photo. His huge hands were good for palming a basketball, spanning chords on a piano, and flicking boogers. Fred has had a very successful career as a musician, and as with many M&Aers, his talent was obvious right from the start.

It's not that everyone who went to Music and Art was that focused. I certainly wasn't, but a lot of students were, with the out-and-out focus king being my classmate Edward Burak.

He's the guy in this yearbook photo with the pipe. He always knew exactly what he wanted to be

Margo Magnus   Agnes Maier   Jonathan Malmude

Robert Mankoff   Edward Burak   Susan Marber

and devoted his life to the aesthetics of the pipe.

Burak collectors, please feel free to contribute

The Art of Edward F. Burak, Dean of American Pipe Designers

Ed Burak is the dean of American pipe designers whose work has had a worldwide influence on the 1943, his first love was painting. His promise as an artist led to a scholarship to the School of Visua

In 1966, needing to have a Meerschaum pipe repaired, he met and subsequently began working with time he produced a small number of Meerschaum pipes, a few of which are still extant in collection: Connoisseur Pipe Shop, where he was able to concentrate on his own designs. Burak's pipes have and Tony Passante. Several of his freehands are in the Museum of Modern Art in New York and ha

Burak's work is best known as pipe design as fine art. He admires pays tribute to the classic Englis with these traditional values yet reflect his own interpretations. He is best know for his freehands, w dollars.

Burak's gallery is the Connoisseur Pipe Shop, Ltd., USB Building, 1285 Avenue of the Americas (co

Recently, prominent figures in the pipe collecting community have applauded Burak's work:

"Edward Burak is a pipe designer. And an artist. A purist, an art instructor, a historian - all held toge with pipes like you have never seen elsewhere. Except, perhaps, in museums ... Burak's work has i in the Museum of Modern Art ....

Ed Burak Connoisseur, courtesy Rob Denholtz

Who knows what I would have become if I had had that type of single-minded focus?

Robert Mankoff

But I didn't. I had no idea of what I wanted to be, although my experience at Music and Art had taught me that one thing I definitely was not going to be was an artist or illustrator. Wasn't good enough. Sure, some of the kids at M&A drew worse than me, but a lot more drew better, and some were incredible draftsmen. And being exposed to real drawing talent made mine wither. I didn't touch a pen, pencil, or paintbrush for three years after graduating. But, as my diploma attests, I did graduate.

So, off I went to Syracuse University, where I devoted myself to the aesthetics of my hair.

Also to being a wise guy—as in Jewish from Queens, not Italian from Little Italy. Aristotle said that wit is a kind of "educated insolence." Some of my own education in this type of insolence came during the sociology final in my junior year at Syracuse University. I was, shall we say, an indifferent student—and my professors from that time would confirm this. That is, if they remember me at all, which would be unlikely because I never went to class, so the only time they saw me was during finals. Once, I overslept and arrived half an hour late for an exam. While grabbing the exam book, I caught the professor's suspicious eye. He came over to my desk and said loudly,

"Who the hell are you?" The class giggled.

I replied, "You know, I could very well ask you the same question."

He laughed hard. The class laughed harder. I flunked. Lesson learned, but not the one he was teaching. What I realized was that the power of humor was more than just the ability to get laughs. It conferred a kind of actual power. It's a commonplace that it's easier for the boss to get a laugh than a subordinate.

"All right, Rogers! I know I made a humorous remark,
but in my opinion you've laughed enough."

In that classroom situation I was certainly the subordinate and the teacher was definitely the boss, until humor reversed the roles.

Incidents like that taught me something else about humor: that it demands a certain chutzpah, the guts to do something, not just think it.

Following that credo, I did some things during those years that were funny clever, some that were funny crazy, and some that were both. Looking back, I think some of my pranks were a kind of performance art before there was performance art. An example:

The student cafeteria at Syracuse had a rule that you had to wear socks, but at the time my preference was for loafers without socks. I solved that problem by using Magic Markers to decorate my bare feet and ankles with a pair of simulated argyle socks.

In my senior year at Syracuse, 1966, a book that would be important to me came out: *Learning to Cartoon*, by Syd Hoff, who most people of a certain age identify with the children's classics *Danny and the Dinosaur* and *Sammy the Seal*. But Hoff was also an accomplished and prolific gag cartoonist who drew hundreds of cartoons for *The New Yorker* and many thousands for other magazines and newspapers. The preface was very encouraging, with genial Syd assuring me how easy the process would be.

PREFACE

Hello, I'm Syd Hoff. Perhaps you've seen some of my cartoons in magazines and newspapers.

Is it hard becoming a cartoonist? No, it isn't. And to prove it I've written this book—and gotten together the work of some of the greatest people in the business to help show you. Here is real fun for you, if you'd like to learn cartooning as an amateur. And if making a professional career of it becomes your ambition, I sincerely believe that you will find some help in these pages too.

The table of contents made it all seem pretty straightforward.

CONTENTS

As did the basic illustrations on composition

Mrs. Brown feels very blue here. It isn't the housework that's got her down—she just knows her composition is all wrong.

See how much better Mrs. Brown feels now. (It's the little things that make women happy!)

and figure drawing, which were as simple as they were sexist.

The Creator used a better blueprint than this (thank God!), but for cartoonistic purposes, our version should suffice. If you need additional reference, perhaps the lady across the street won't draw her blind tonight.

I worked hard all that year to produce twenty-seven cartoons. Twenty-seven, count 'em. I know I did, because I was so impressed with the number. I figured these would soon be published, providing vast amounts of income and laurels on which I could comfortably rest before creating another year's worth. What were those cartoons of mine like? Here are a couple of examples sketched from memory.

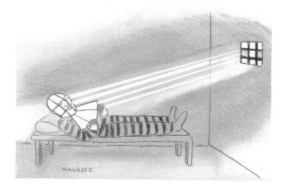

"Hey honey, did you know if you hold a glass up to your ear you can hear the sink?"

I confidently took them around to the magazines of that time that featured cartoons, like *The Saturday Evening Post, Look,* and *Esquire,* though not *The New Yorker. The New Yorker* would not see you in person, whereas the cartoon editors of these other magazines would. And I wanted my genius to be validated in person. The editors were very nice but nevertheless rejected all twenty-seven—count 'em—of my cartoons. They did, however, encourage me to come back with more. More? How could anyone do more than twenty-seven cartoons? With my genius insulted—in person, no less—I quit cartooning to see what else I might be suited for, only before I could find out, the United States government determined that I was suited for combat in Vietnam. So I determined that I needed to get a deferment.

Look, I was as patriotic as the next guy, so long as the next guy was a draft dodger. My first dodge was to get a job as a welfare worker, which at the time provided you with a temporary deferment. In my case very temporary, because I was so bad at it that I got fired and became temporarily eligible for welfare myself. I also once again became eligible for the military, but I didn't like the short-hair thing or the killing thing—which was bad—or the dying thing, which was worse.

My father, Lou Mankoff, had served honorably in the Big One, where millions had died. He tried to convince me that my apprehensions were overwrought about this Smaller One, where mere thousands were perishing. He pointed out that I might not be sent to Vietnam; that even if I was, I might not see combat; that even if I did, I might not get shot; that even if was shot . . . He didn't finish that part because I told him I was going to Canada. But I didn't, because he had something else up his sleeve: a graduate school deferment. Great idea, except I couldn't get into graduate school because my grades were so poor. No problem: the ever-resourceful Lou removed from his sleeve a newspaper ad, which proclaimed, in huge print, "WE WILL GET YOU INTO GRADUATE SCHOOL IN TWO WEEKS!" And in much smaller print: "for $300."

Shortly thereafter I walked into the graduate psychology program at Atlanta University, in Georgia, an all-black school except, now, for me.

I roomed with a guy from Ghana, name of Agyenim Boateng, who was outraged by how whites treated blacks in this country and sometimes told me that blacks should "burn the country down." Other than that, he really was a very reasonable fellow and, even though I was white, never tried to set me on fire. In later years he mellowed, became a United States citizen, a Republican, and eventually the deputy attorney general of Kentucky, where, as far as I know, he strictly enforced the laws against arson.

Being white down in the black section of Atlanta in the late 1960s was an interesting experience. Atlanta was the home of SNCC (Student Nonviolent Coordinating Committee), and I was sometimes mistaken for one of the few whites involved in the organization. One time at a diner that, unbeknownst to me, was a SNCC gathering place, Stokely Carmichael came up to me (without the microphones) and asked me if I was Frank. I

said, "No, I'm Bob, but right on anyway, brother." What was this radical firebrand's response? He laughed. My education in insolence continued.

After sometimes being mistaken for someone else and sometimes being mistaken for a psychology student, I transferred from Atlanta University to Fairleigh Dickinson University, where I got a master's in experimental psychology, and then to the City University of New York, where I came oh so close to getting a PhD. Here's my transcript to prove it:

When, after I'd spent two years in the program, my experimental animal died (and not from laughter, I might add), I took it as an omen to quit.

"You can't miss it. Take a right and two lefts."

Besides, something was drawing my attention away from psychology: drawing. I had never completely stopped drawing cartoons, even while in graduate school, and my fizzling psychology career reignited my passion for it.

Ironically, decades later I would return to psychology to study what made people, not animals, laugh. But back then, I knew that quitting would disappoint my Jewish mother, who was hoping she could one day exclaim, "My son, the doctorate!"

I tried persuading her that I was merely switching from one "ology" to another. Instead of being a psychologist, I would be a cartoonologist.

She told me that whatever I wanted to be was fine with her, even if it was a garbageman—so long, she specified, as I was the best garbageman.

Eventually I convinced her that becoming a cartoonist was less of a long shot than being the top garbageman in a city with more than eleven thousand sanitation workers.

My father was a tougher case. When he heard I wanted to be a cartoonist, he solemnly declared, "You know, they already have people who do that." He was right, of course. There were no signs in *The New Yorker* indicating a shortage of cartoonists.

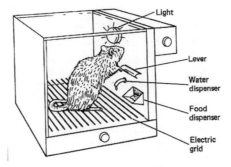

HELP WANTED: CARTOONIST NEEDED

Jokingly, I pointed out that one of them might die; I would scan the obits for this event and, when it happened, seize the opportunity, pop up at *The New Yorker*'s offices, portfolio in hand, ready to begin my glorious cartooning career. To which he replied,

"You're joking, right?"

"Right, that's why I should be a cartoonist."

Only what would be required to accomplish that goal was not a *New Yorker* cartoonist obit vigil but persistence, a lesson I'd learned as an animal behaviorist doling out rewards and punishments to helpless critters in ways that are now outlawed by both the American Psychological Association and the Geneva Conventions.

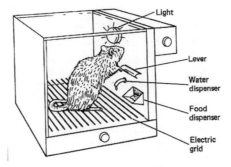

The reward-and-punishment theory being applied to the rodent above had relevance to the Robert on the next page.

These experiments taught me that consistent rewards do not encourage the persistent habits you need to make it as a cartoonist.

Mankoff, circa 1974

You would think that rewarding an animal every time it performs a desired act would be the best way to instill a habit. Rewarding that way is known as a continuous reinforcement schedule. The problem is that the habit quickly disappears when the rewards stop. In behavioral jargon this is called "extinction." A rat rewarded with food every time he presses the bar has a fit if the reward is withheld. He sulks, pouts, and then stops.

On the other hand, you can train animals to be very persistent by rewarding them on what are called intermittent schedules of reinforcement. Sometimes a reward occurs after one response, sometimes after 10 or 16 or 112 or 1,012. Schedule it right and these animals are hooked for life.

And, by analogy, that's what happened to me. I began selling cartoons to a variety of magazines, including *Saturday Review*

"Elementary, my dear Watson: the cartoonist did it."

and *National Lampoon*.

"Quick! Hide! That may be my husband!"

The editors, it turns out, were subjecting me to the same intermittent reinforcement schedule I'd used on the rats. Here I am, not realizing the Skinner box I have gotten myself into, hooked just like my rats on the intermittent rewards, not of food pellets but of selling cartoons.

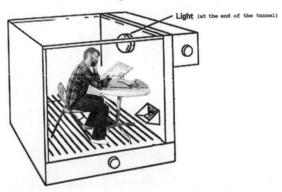

At this point in my quest for cartoon success, my father had taken to bragging to his friends, "They laughed when my son said he was going to be a cartoonist, but they're not laughing now." I had to remind him that I wanted them to be laughing—but one magazine, *The New Yorker*, still wasn't.

After two years of submitting, all I had to show for it were enough *New Yorker* rejection slips to wallpaper my bathroom.

Undaunted, and financially sustained by the sales to other magazines, I kept at it. Besides, I had other rooms that needed wallpaper.

CHAPTER THREE

A BRIEF HISTORY
OF CARTOONING

W hy was I so obsessed with getting published in *The New Yorker*? Well, it would be a big boost to my ego, which at that point, publication in other magazines notwithstanding, needed some boosting. *The New Yorker* was and is the Everest of magazine cartooning. Scaling that mountain would mean that I was a SUCCESS! Which would be especially appealing when contrasted with my prior FAILURES! In addition to the welfare and psychology fiascos, I had also flopped at trying to teach speed-reading to Catholic high school girls, urging them to read faster or they would burn in hell.

There was also a practical reason for zeroing in on *The New Yorker*. If I was going to be a real cartoonist, I was going to have to earn a living at it. Maybe not a great living but enough to put a roof over my head and a shag rug on the floor (it was the 1970s, remember).

The New Yorker paid the most for a cartoon: $300. That is the equivalent of about $1,300 today. If you sold twenty cartoons a year, you could scrape by—with the help of periodic grants from the Mollie and Lou Mankoff Foundation.

And I really did want to earn a living as a cartoonist, if only to allow my parents to answer in the affirmative when their nosy friends asked, "Can he make a living at that?" Even after all these years, I still get that same question—and, more pointedly, the inquiry about what *The New Yorker* pays for cartoons. I say I'm happy to tell my questioner if they're happy telling me how much money they make. Usually they're not.

But, to be honest, the real root of my obsession with *The New Yorker* lay in its historic role in the development of the magazine cartoon. That's how it is for many cartoonists, and even noncartoonists, like the late film critic Roger Ebert, who wrote this on his blog:

> I have entered the *New Yorker*'s Cartoon Caption Contest almost weekly virtually since it began and have never even been a finalist. Mark Twain advised: "Write without pay until somebody offers to pay you. If nobody offers within three years, sawing wood is what you were intended for." I have done more writing for free for the *New Yorker* in the last five years than for anybody in the previous 40 years.
>
> It's not that I think my cartoon captions are better than anyone else's, although some weeks, understandably, I do. It's that just *once* I want to see one of my damn captions in the magazine that publishes the best cartoons in the world.

By the way, in 2011 Ebert finally won, after 107 tries.

"The best cartoons in the world": my sentiment exactly. But there was something more, because the cartoons were cheek by jowl with the best articles by the best writers. Damn, *The New Yorker* even had the best type font, Adobe Caslon, which I'm using here. *The New Yorker* was the complete package, its great cartoons the perfect complement to its brilliant articles—or from my cartoon-obsessed perspective, the other way around.

Look, I was born in the Bronx and grew up in the 1950s, when the Yankees were winning one World Series after another. To me *The New Yorker* was to cartooning what the New York Yankees were to baseball—the Best Team. If you could make that team, you too were one of the best.

As a kid, I actually fantasized about becoming a Yankee. It would be Maris in right field, the Mick in center, and the Mankoff in left. Well, that was never going to happen, but if I could make *The New Yorker* cartoon team and take the field alongside

Saul Steinberg,

Peter Arno,

"Now read me the part again where I disinherit everybody."

and James Thurber,

"It's a naïve domestic Burgundy without any breeding,
but I think you'll be amused by its presumption."

that would do just fine.

These and other *New Yorker* cartoonists didn't invent the magazine cartoon, but they did revolutionize it. All revolutions need a bit of history to be understood, so I hope you'll tolerate a brief lesson.

The honor of inventing the magazine cartoon, and also inadvertently appropriating the word "cartoon" to mean a humorous illustration, goes to the British magazine *Punch*, which way back the middle of the nineteenth century started it all with this drawing:

SUBSTANCE AND SHADOW.

It's labeled "CARTOON, No. 1," which would be pretty clever if *Punch* wanted credit for creating the first cartoon, because, after all, it's right there telling you it is No. 1. But that's not the real story, because "cartoon" didn't mean then what it means now. Then it meant a preliminary sketch for a painting. *Punch* was mockingly suggesting that its sketch go into a contest to determine which high-toned paintings would adorn the Houses of Parliament. I won't try to exhume the humor of this illustration, except to say that there was some, it was satiric, and you had to be there in England in 1843 to get it. Since none of us were, let's move on. Anyway, *Punch* published more in a similar vein, calling them "cartoons," and the name stuck.

By 1899, when this *Punch* cartoon

THE POINT OF VIEW.
Exasperated old gentleman (to lady in front of him).
"Excuse me, madam, but my seat has cost me ten shillings, and I want to see. Your hat—" The lady: "My hat has cost me ten guineas, sir, and I want it to be seen!"

was published, a cartoon definitely meant a drawn joke, though to us the joke just seems drawn out. It was probably a knee-slapper back when big hats on ladies and exasperated old codgers were de rigueur. Anyway, let's give credit where credit is due—it's definitely an improvement, to our modern eyes, on *Substance and Shadow*.

Cartoons on this side of the Atlantic, like these from *Life*, aped the *Punch* model, producing, if not gales of laughter, perhaps an occasional wheeze, which over time turned to a yawn, as the formula ran out of steam in the 1920s.

He: "BEASTLY SNOBS, THOSE VAN GRUNTS, I BOWED TO THEM.
BUT THEY CUT ME DEAD."
She: "NEVER MIND, HERE ARE THE SMITHS, LET'S CUT THEM;
THEY'VE TRIED TO BOW TO US."

She: "YOU CAN'T BUY MY LOVE!"
He: "BUT YOU DON'T KNOW HOW MUCH MONEY I'VE GOT."

Which is when *The New Yorker* came to the rescue, shaking to bits the old overdrawn, underfunny illustrated dialogue cartoon and replacing it with humor that was quick and visual and whose captions sounded the way Americans spoke.

But that shake-up took a while to get shook. When *The New Yorker* was founded, in 1925, proclaiming that it would be distinguished for its cartoons, it really wasn't. The images were as stiff as those that had gone before, and the language just as stilted.

"The man who marries my daughter will win a prize."
"Well, I must say that's awfully sporting of you."

Visitor: Who's the old boy going out?
Member: He's had tough luck. His wife ran away about a year ago.
Then he lost a ball in the rough and that seemed too much for him.

Something more direct, natural, funny, and sassy was needed. A step in the right direction was taken in this famous and beloved cartoon from 1929, with drawing by Carl Rose and a caption provided by E. B. White.

"It's broccoli, dear."
"I say it's spinach, and I say the hell with it."

The incongruity of the little girl willfully and, for that time, somewhat vulgarly ignoring the facts to indulge her own wrongheadedness struck a nerve with the public, and the phrase "I say it's spinach and the hell with it" became a catchphrase, basically meaning "don't confuse me with the facts, I'll do what like." It was also adapted into a hit song by Irving Berlin.

Long as there's you, long as there's me
Long as the best things in life are free
I say it's spinach and the hell with it
The hell with it, that's all!

The cartoon was still well enough known in 2012 that when the debate over the constitutionality of Obamacare reached the Supreme Court and Justice Antonin Scalia wondered aloud whether, if the government could force you to buy health care, it could also make you eat broccoli, I was able to reference it with this cartoon.

"I say it's government-mandated broccoli, and I say the hell with it."

However, I shortened the caption to one line, because beloved or not, the original still followed the same old two-line dialogue formula. And while the drawing has more zip than those ponderous ones from *Punch*, it's really E. B. White's verbal punch that makes it work.

Perhaps the ultimate coup de grâce, both in style and substance, to the old two-line formula was provided by James Thurber, who in one fell swoop, in 1932, pared the caption down to not just a single line but a single word.

"Touché!"

This perfect melding of an enigmatic image in need of humorous clarification by a one-line caption became the hallmark of *New Yorker* cartoons. The best of these functioned as mini comic theater, complete with actors, sets, and props, with the right caption kicking it all home.

"I can't smell a thing either."

The caption of the following cartoon, by Peter Arno, from 1941, joined "I say it's spinach and I say the hell with it" as a contribution to the American vernacular. "Back to the drawing board" was not a cliché before this cartoon was published.

"Well, back to the old drawing board."

Arno's great caption is now a standard response to any situation that does not turn out as planned. It aptly described the situation I was in. My frontal assault on Fortress *New Yorker* had not gotten me in, and I was back at the drawing board, looking for inspiration to keep my aspiration alive.

CHAPTER FOUR

DECONSTRUCTING *NEW YORKER* CARTOONS

Determined to educate myself on what a *New Yorker* cartoon was, and what mine weren't, I took myself off to the New York Public Library. There, the collected volumes of *The New Yorker* included every issue, and therefore every cartoon, published up until that time. I planned to look at all of them. There was some familial precedent to this quest because of the role the library had played in my father's education.

He grew up on a Lower East Side straight out of *Hester Street*. He had little formal education, having left school in the eighth grade to help support his family. But you wouldn't know it to talk to him. Impressed with his erudition on a wide range of topics, people would often ask him where he'd gone to college. He always answered, wryly and proudly, "The New York Public Library."

Here I was, decades later, using the library as my cartoon college, bent on becoming not only a cartoonist but, as I had half-facetiously told my mother, also a cartoonologist, scientifically (or at least pseudoscientifically) investigating the variables that made *New Yorker* cartoons what they were. And as I marched through the decades from the 1920s up to the 1970s, looking for the path to *New Yorker* cartoonhood, I had an epiphany: there was no such thing as a typical *New Yorker* cartoon. They could have very short captions

"Curiosity."

or very long ones

"Edgar, please run down to the shopping center right away, and get some milk and cat food. Don't get canned tuna, or chicken, or liver, or any of those awful combinations. Shop around and get a surprise. The pussies like surprises."

or none at all.

The humor could be whimsical,

"I don't know. George got it somewhere."

satirical,

"Aren't you being a little arrogant, son? Here's Lieutenant Colonel Farrington, Major Stark, Caption Truelove, Lieutenant Castle, and myself, all older and more experienced than you, and we think the war is very moral."

philosophical,

	1	2	3	4	5	6	7	8	9	**TOTAL**
REALISTS	2	0	1	4	2	1	0	6	2	0
IDEALISTS	0	0	0	0	0	0	0	0	0	1

D. FRADON

or just interesting.

I later learned that *The New Yorker* doesn't call a cartoon a cartoon. The material of interest is referred to as a "drawing." And because it's a drawing, not a cartoon, it doesn't necessarily have to be funny. Interesting is enough, if you're as interesting as William Steig

or Saul Steinberg.

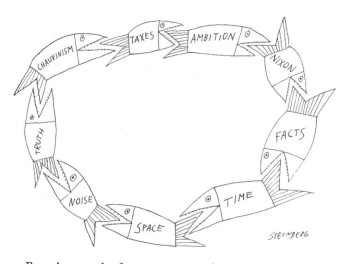

But whatever the form or content of the cartoons, the one common thread that ran through all of those I studied in the New York Public Library was that they made the reader think.

FISH
Saul Steinberg, Untitled, 1958; Ink on paper, 11 ½ x 14 ½ in.; Beinecke Rare Book and Manuscript Library, Yale University
Originally published in The New Yorker, December 20, 1958.; © The Saul Steinberg Foundation/Artists Rights Society (ARS), New York

COGITO
Saul Steinberg, Untitled, 1962; Ink on paper
Originally published in The New Yorker, December 22, 1962.; © The Saul Steinberg Foundation/Artists Rights Society (ARS), New York

You had to be a participant in the experience, up-to-date on the latest trends and buzzwords, aware of the world around you, and possessing a mental flexibility able to appreciate different comic visions, techniques, and talents.

Two of those talents, Saul Steinberg and James Thurber, particularly inspired me; Steinberg appealed to my rationality and Thurber to my whimsicality.

Steinberg's cartoons didn't cause an outward laugh or even an inward one, but they made my mind smile. Each one was a philosophical mediation in ink.

ART
Saul Steinberg, Untitled, 1960; Ink on paper, 14 ½ x 23 in.; Beinecke Rare Book and Manuscript Library, Yale University;
Originally published in The New Yorker, July 2, 1960.; © The Saul Steinberg Foundation/Artists Rights Society (ARS), New York

Cartoons like this resonated with me because many of the cartoons I was doing were also "concept" cartoons; their aim was to be intellectually amusing rather than simply funny.

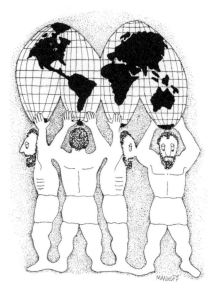

Thurber provided a different kind of inspiration—actually, two kinds. First, his flavor of funny wasn't like the traditional gag.

His captions didn't make sense of the image. Instead, the caption made what was going on stranger and, if you were on the Thurber wavelength, funnier.

"That's my first wife up there, and this is the <u>present</u> Mrs. Harris."

"I brought a couple of midgets—do you mind?"

Thurber's jokes were not the type you "get" in that classic way where you suddenly put two different frames of reference together and therefore are able to understand why the former Mrs. Harris is up there on the bookshelf. And trying to figure out where the midgets came from or, for that matter, why they made you giggle, wasn't going to get you anywhere. It was go-with-the-flow humor in which you enjoyed absurdity by giving yourself over to it.

That approach appealed to my wacky side and encouraged me to, well, have a whack at it. My absurdity was different from Thurber's because weirdness by definition, if truly weird, needs to be idiosyncratic.

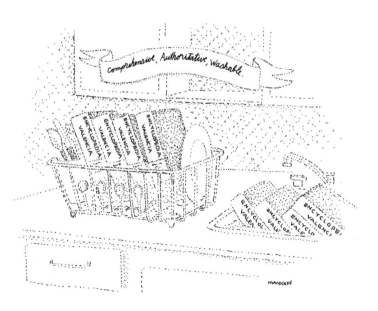

"Good work, Bevans, but in this business climate I've got to ask myself the question 'Is a choreography department absolutely essential?'"

Though none of these made it into *The New Yorker*, a few of their quirky brethren eventually got there.

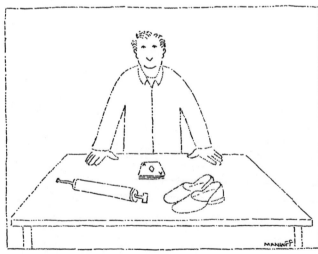

"All you need is a bicycle pump, an ordinary deck of playing cards, and a pair of deerskin slippers, and you're ready to begin."

Suddenly a delightful Continental custom is sweeping America!

The second way Thurber inspired me was, paradoxically, by his apparent lack of drawing ability. Look, if the requirement for admission to *The New Yorker* was that I would have to draw as well as Addams, Arno, George Price,

"Watch out, Fred! Here it comes again!"

or Charles Saxon,

"What would you do if you had a million dollars—tax-free, I mean?"

well, that was going to be too high a bar for someone who couldn't even make the Music and Art honor roll. But Thurber's drawing ability was considerably less daunting. It looked amateurish by any academic standard, including that of my old high school. In fact, to get into M&A I'd had to submit a portfolio that included drawings of the human figure, and if those figures had looked anything like Thurber's homunculi, I never would have been admitted.

When a critic once said Thurber was a "fifth-rate" artist, *The New Yorker*'s editor, Harold Ross, wryly corrected him: "Third-rate." But that third-rate drawing style produced some of *The New Yorker*'s most memorable cartoons.

"All right, have it your way—you heard a seal bark!"

"Well, it makes a difference to me!"

What I needed was a style as suited to my ideas as Thurber's was to his.

CHAPTER FIVE

FINDING MY STYLE

I actually tried the Thurber approach early on. This was the first cartoon I ever sold, to *Saturday Review* in 1974—just a minimalist line drawing employing my very own homunculi.

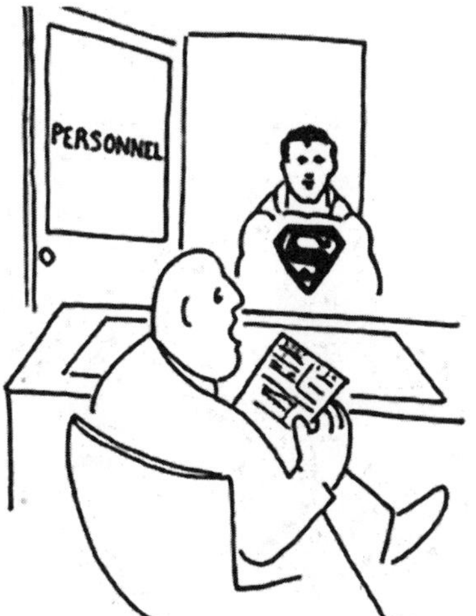
PERSONNEL

"Faster than a speeding bullet . . . More powerful than a locomotive . . . No shorthand?"

Here's another early one. But now, besides lines, another feature had crept in. Dots.

"My main fear used to be cats—now it's carcinogens."

I might say I eventually found my style by connecting the dots; however, the opposite was the case.

Creating images using dots, or stippling, had a long tradition in illustration but none in cartooning. I've always thought that "stippling" sounds sort of like a dermatological disease.

"Bad news, Mr. Mankoff—this is the worst case of stippling I've ever seen."

I did have a pretty bad case of it, going back to my time at Music and Art. There, in a History of Art class, I'd come in contact with the work of the impressionist Georges Seurat, who'd created his paintings in a style called pointillism.

Now, that seemed a crazy way to paint or draw, though maybe not so crazy, because when I looked at photographs in magazines and newspapers, I saw that when enlarged, they were actually made up of tiny dots. So I started using dots to make my own distorted versions of them.

At that time, it was just a type of dot doodling of photograph-inspired faces.

This eventually morphed into my cartoon style.

Even though drawing cartoons this way took a long time, it did have its advantages. First, since no one had ever drawn cartoons using this style, it was certain to get the attention of editors. Generally, I think this worked in my favor, although I remember receiving a note from one editor saying my ideas were good, but could I redraw them in a less cumbersome style? Only when I did that, it turned out that the ideas weren't good enough. Damn editors, impossible to please. I know, now that I'm one of them.

I created the dots with this instrument, a technical drawing pen called a Rapidograph. It was certainly ironically named,

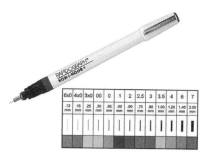

as far as I was concerned, because the time it took me to do a cartoon with it was anything but rapid.

In this cartoon, using the tiniest pen tip available, I created every tone from lightest gray to blackest black with tiny dots.

"Please tell the king, I've remembered the punch line."

Honestly, the style was a pain in the neck. Eventually I had to modify it because of real physical pains, but when I was starting out, in addition to getting the attention of editors, it had another advantage: it forced me to be at the drawing board for many hours. A cartoon like this would take a whole dotting day. Which was okay, because time spent drawing

was time not spent doing something else. Time in which I could meditate, cogitate, and create until I came up with another idea.

Sometimes I would stare at a small section of the drawing and the dots would seem to dance and shimmer.

I would space out into a kind of focused trance where my hand was doing one thing on the drawing board and my mind was busy conceptualizing, dreaming up cartoons that, I hoped, would be as intellectually ambitious in their own way as Steinberg's were in his.

Certainly they were intellectual. I may be the only cartoonist ever to make a joke about Kurt Godel's incompleteness theorems of mathematics.

"The arithmetic seems correct yet I find myself haunted by the idea that the basic axioms on which the arithmetic is based might give rise to contradictions which would then invalidate these computations."

Looking back, I think I was trying to prove to my parents, and also myself, that even though I hadn't made it through graduate school in experimental psychology, I was now doing postdoc work as an experimental cartoonist.

I was systematically, if not consciously, experimenting with the parameters of the cartoon format, sometimes using no words and being silly

and sometimes using lots of them to make an ironic point.

"O.K. guys, let's have a good clean fight. No racial epithets, ethnic slurs, or disparaging remarks about place of national origin. No derogation of religious persuasion, political affiliation, or sexual orientation. In case of a knockdown go immediately to a neutral corner and refrain from any taunts, jeers, or gibes about pugilistic ability."

But whether being brainy

MANKOFF

Tomb of the Unknown Quantity.

or zany,

MANKOFF

Macho Vegetarian

I was at the drawing board for hours, developing the technique of looking at an idea from many different angles, which would then reveal even more angles.

Each idea would spawn variations on a theme that I would exhaust until it exhausted me. And whenever I became obsessed with something besides cartooning, the two forces would combine. In the early 1970s, after Bobby Fischer became world champion, my obsession with chess combined with my cartoon obsession to produce this obsessive cartoon chess riff:

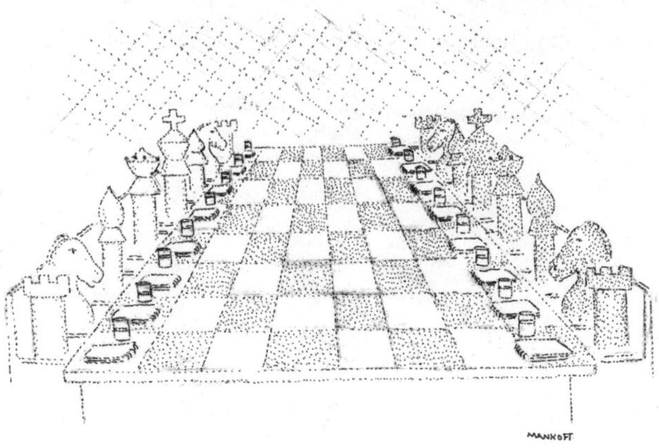
MANKOFF

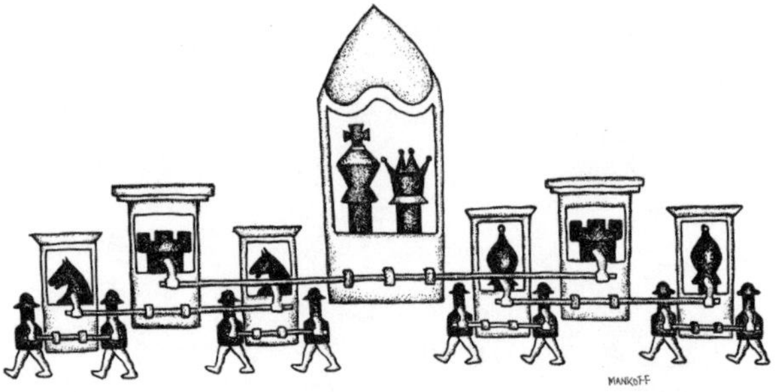
MANKOFF

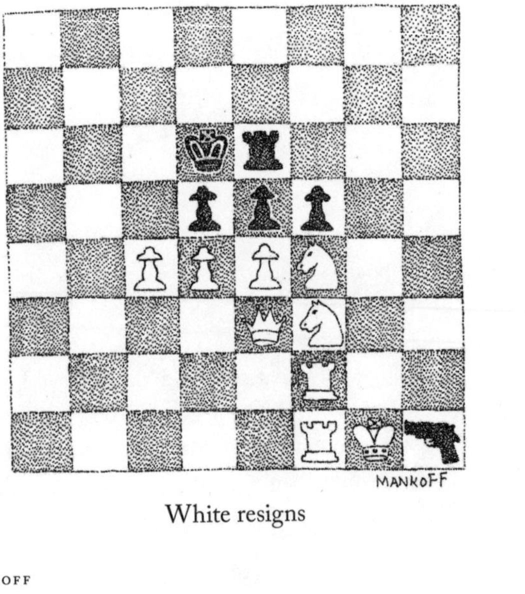
MANKOFF

White resigns

Which I probably would have been better off submitting to a chess magazine than to *The New Yorker*, although *The New Yorker* did publish the cartoon below at the time of Fischer's triumph over the Russian Boris Spassky, when for a brief moment chess became a spectator sport.

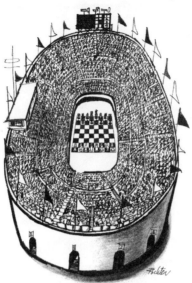

I finally did get a chess cartoon in *The New Yorker* in 1997, when the IBM computer Deep Blue beat the reigning world chess champion, Garry Kasparov.

"No, I don't want to play chess. I just want you to reheat the lasagna."

Compared to my attempts of decades earlier, I guess it had the advantage of actually being funny.

So varying the variations became my modus operandi, and I used the method to operate on themes as varied as logic and hand shadows.

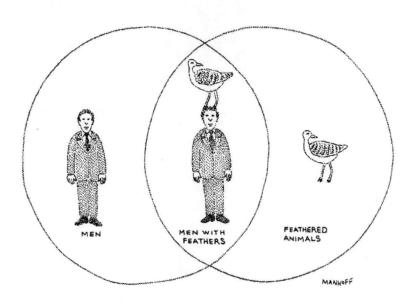

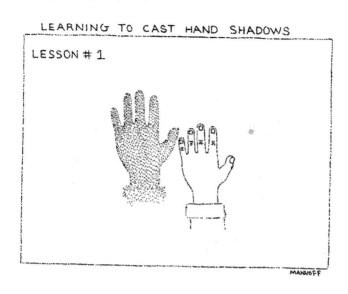

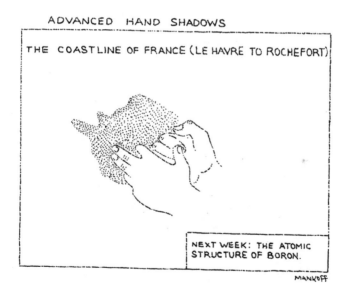

Sometimes, the variations between cartoons would be relatively minor, as with these two explorations on man-and-machine interactions using an old-fashioned printing press.

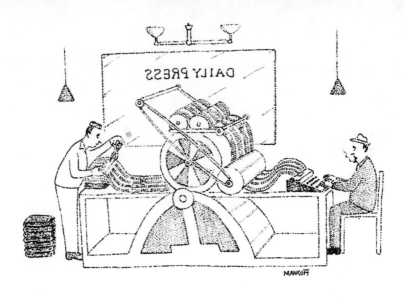

Not that much difference between the two, right? But whatever the difference was, it was difference enough, because after two thousand submissions, *The New Yorker* bought the second one.

And then this rejection slip

We regret that we are unable
to use the enclosed material.
Thank you for giving us the
opportunity to consider it.

The Editors

magically changed to this:

Hey! You sold one. No
shit! You really sold a
cartoon to the fucking
New Yorker magazine.

The Editors

Okay, that's not what really happened. There is a *New Yorker* rejection
slip, but there's no acceptance slip. And if there were one, that certainly
wouldn't be it.

CHAPTER SIX

MY GENERATION

The way I actually found out that I had finally sold a cartoon to *The New Yorker* was by the appearance of an inconspicuous little "o" scribbled in pencil on the back of that drawing by the art editor, Lee Lorenz. When I called the office to find out what this meant I was told by his assistant, Anne Hall, that the "o" stood for "O.K." and that they would now like me to do a "finish" on the drawing. This confused me. I said it was already finished, that's why I'd handed it in—it was done. But Anne explained to me that what cartoonists handed in for consideration were called "roughs," which, if bought, then were redrawn and called "finishes." Clearly, if cartooning is ever to get the respect it deserves, it's going to need fancier jargon. Anyway, it turns out that all they wanted was for me to remove the background, which, with the miracle of Wite-Out, I did, and—voilà!—to my delight and my parents' astonishment, on June 20, 1977, that cartoon appeared in *The New Yorker*.

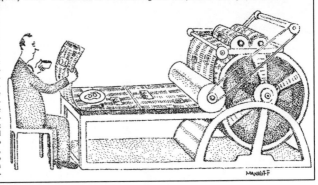

I was part of the new crew of young—or at least youngish—cartoonists that Lee Lorenz, my predecessor as cartoon editor, brought into the magazine in the 1970s. Having arrived before me was Jack Ziegler, and quickly following were Mick Stevens, Michael Maslin, and Roz Chast. We're the old—or at least oldish—guard now, but our memories of that first cartoon sale are still fresh. Before I continue my memoiring, it might be nice to take a break and include their memories of that delicious moment when they sold their first cartoon.

MICK STEVENS:

In San Francisco, where I lived back in the seventies before getting a foothold at *The New Yorker,* I would sit for hours at the drawing board waiting for inspiration in front of that "blazing white island"—which the cartoonist Bill Woodman once called the blank pieces of paper we eventually draw on. (He was quoting James Dickey, I think.)

I was a fan of country-and-western music at the time, but I was living with a woman who played the classical violin. She had introduced me to Bach, Beethoven, and Mozart, and now I was whistling "Eine Kleine Nachtmusik" around the house instead of "Honky Tonk Blues." I had a tape recording of the Mozart piece, which for a while was always playing on my old cassette player behind me as I drew my weekly batch of ideas. One day while I was listening and doodling as usual, I found myself drawing an empty frame, then a horizon line within it. I added a few forlorn-looking clouds above the horizon, then some random objects in the foreground: an old tire, a tin can, an empty bottle, a pencil, and assorted debris. I stared at this melancholy scene for a while, then added a box at the top for a potential title. I was stuck there for a while and was about to give up on that particular germ of an idea. Then, a few minutes later, I heard "Eine Kleine Nachtmusik" suddenly stop playing behind me, followed by the sad, crunching sound those old tapes made as they died, eaten by the cassette player's hungry mechanism. It was suddenly very quiet in the room. The tape had obviously reached the end of its life.

This event provided me with the title I had been looking for. As it turned out, "Life Without Mozart" became my first O.K. at *The New Yorker.*

JACK ZIEGLER:

Shortly before Christmas of 1973, on my regular stop at *The New Yorker* to drop off new material and pick up last week's returns and rejection slips, I was surprised to find an almost illegible note clipped to my sheaf of that week's losers: "Dear Mr. Ziegler, would you mind stopping back to discuss one of your ideas with me? Thank you."

It was unsigned, but I knew it was from Lee Lorenz, the art editor. After having the note verified by Natasha, the dark, smoldering vixen who was moonlighting as a receptionist, I was let in.

It had been below freezing that morning when I'd left my apartment, so I had on a heavy sweater, topped by a wool sport jacket. By noon, however, the temperature had soared, and perspiration was now dripping off me. I nervously took my seat in the anteroom alongside several other gentlemen: "real" cartoonists (as opposed to me, the neophyte)—all easygoing guys who, unlike me, were quite comfortable hanging out there.

When Lee invited me into his office, he made no mention of my addled appearance; nor did he inquire after my apparently questionable state of health. I sat in the chair opposite him as he pulled my drawing from a fat pile of other people's work on his desk. It was a cartoon that had made me happy when I came up with the idea. Lee asked if I wouldn't mind if they bought it for the magazine and if I'd be amenable to considering a few changes. That was my first exposure to the extremely polite ways of *The New Yorker* in conducting business with its contributors.

The caption and layout were fine, he said, but some adjustments would be required in the body of the drawing. Could I perhaps make the fellow on the phone older and a tad more biblical? And the inner workings of the conveyor belt seemed, well, not quite mechanical enough. Just a few lines added to the finished drawing should do it.

"Hello? Beasts of the Field? This is Lou, over in Birds of the Air. Anything funny going on over at your end?"

Two weeks later I received a check for $305, the largest payment and oddest amount I had yet received for any cartoon sale. One month later, when I was paid for a second drawing the magazine had bought, I was shocked to find that my "regular" fee had been reduced to $215.

"Surely there must be some mistake," I sobbed to Lee over the phone the next day. After a minute or two, he figured out my problem and told me about "the formula." *The New Yorker*, I learned, paid strictly by the square inch—i.e., the amount of space a drawing would take up when it got published in the magazine. (P.S. The formula by which the payment for cartoons is determined has since been changed but cannot be revealed, as it is considered a proprietary trade secret. When I became cartoon editor, I suggested that it be by the dot. Suffice to say that this suggestion was not taken.—R. M.)

MICHAEL MASLIN:

On the Ides of March 1978, I brought in yet another batch of cartoons to the magazine. I'd been submitting for seven years (since I was sixteen years old) with no success, although I'd sold an idea to

The New Yorker a year earlier—an idea eventually executed by Whitney Darrow Jr. Here's the drawing I submitted:

"nothing will ever happen to you."

And here is the published version, drawn by Darrow:

"Nothing will ever happen to you."

I produced the panel in a style in which you rapidly sketch a subject without ever looking down at your drawing pad, which accounts for the fact that it looks as though I never looked down at my drawing pad.

Whitney Darrow's version showed that he clearly did. Good for him, although I sort of felt that was cheating.

Nevertheless, I was proud that my idea had at least gotten into *The New Yorker.* My goal, however, was not to supply established cartoonists with ideas but to see my own drawings published.

That March, I'd gone uptown to the magazine's offices, then located at 25 West 43rd Street, dropped off a new batch of cartoons, and retrieved last week's rejected submissions. Back home in my apartment, I looked through the envelope of rejected work and discovered that one cartoon was missing—this one:

"I'll have a quarter pound of your most reliable cheese."

I didn't think it was the strongest drawing in the batch. As there was no note explaining its absence, and thinking perhaps it had fallen behind a filing cabinet or something, I decided to call the magazine.

Anne Hall, the assistant to Lee Lorenz, the art editor, told me that the drawing probably was misplaced, and . . . well, would I hold while she looked into it? When Anne came back on the line, she said, "Mr. Maslin, I'm sorry, the drawing wasn't misplaced—they bought it."

I said, "They bought it? The whole thing?" ("The whole thing?" was in reference to the previous purchase—you know, when they just bought the idea.)

Anne replied, "Yes, the whole thing."

ROZ CHAST:

I remember the first time I sold a cartoon to *The New Yorker* very clearly. It happened in April 1978. I had graduated from college in May 1977, and in the months in between those two dates, I was taking an illustration portfolio around to various magazines. I had been doing cartoons on and off since I was a kid, but I didn't think anyone would like them, because they were very personal and peculiar. I thought I would have better luck with illustration. I sold a couple of illustrations, but at a certain point, I thought: *This isn't really so great, so I might as well try doing what I want to do*—which was cartoons. My parents were longtime subscribers to *The New Yorker*, so I knew that they used cartoons. I didn't know anything else, like names of editors, how one submitted cartoons, or how many to submit. I called up the offices to find out when their drop-off day was. It was Wednesday. I got together a large number of cartoons—I'm guessing around fifty or sixty—and put them in one of those brown envelopes, the kind with the elastic band around it. I didn't have any expectations whatsoever of selling a cartoon. I dropped my cartoons off at the transom. When I came back for my portfolio the next week, there was a note inside that I couldn't read. I asked the somewhat alarming red-haired lady who sat at the transom desk to translate. It said, "Please see me. Lee." I asked who Lee was. She said he was Lee Lorenz, the art editor, and buzzed me in. I walked down a hallway to his office, where I have a vague memory of a lot of old guys standing around. I was very, very, very, very anxious. I went in to see Lee, and he told me that they were buying a cartoon. I was pretty flabbergasted. It was, in many ways, the most peculiar and personal of the lot: *Little Things*.

I think I was too shocked to show any emotions on the surface. Lee asked me if I was glad, and I said yes. We talked a little while, I can't remember about what. Here's a horrible memory: after they bought this one, I actually asked him if he would like to take another look at the huge pile of cartoons I'd submitted, if perhaps there was another one in there that he had missed. Cringe-o-rama. He kind of laughed. He told me to keep coming back every week and explained a little about how it worked. That's what I've been doing ever since, more or less.

Let's look at these "firsts" as a group:

"I'll have a quarter pound of your most reliable cheese."

"Hello? Beasts of the Field? This is Lou, over in Birds of the Air. Anything funny going on at your end?"

They are all sort of strange, with Roz's being so strange as to make the others look normal. And, except for Ziegler's, they are as likely to produce puzzlement as amusement. Certainly my early efforts seemed more like whimsical puzzles than jokes. Probably, each one of us wondered why this one was picked rather than all the others, and why this one opened the gates to the promised land.

I think the answer lies with what Lee Lorenz, who in 1973 had become art editor (it wasn't called cartoon editor then), was looking for. What he wasn't looking for was what he already had, although what he had was plenty good: an established crew of cartoonists he had inherited from the previous art editor, James Geraghty.

However, if Lorenz was going to have a legacy other than Geraghty's, he was going to have to develop his own crew. And the members of that crew couldn't just be replacements for the old guard, turning out their imitations of cartoons that the old guard was already doing.

Lee also needed something else, because the way cartoons were being created was changing. In the 1930s, '40s, and '50s, it was common for gag writers to supply the ideas for cartoons. In fact, Geraghty broke into the magazine supplying ideas for Peter Arno, and even after he became editor he continued to do so. The writer James Reid Parker was the caption collaborator for virtually all the lines of Helen Hokinson's stout matrons.

"I hope this isn't going to emphasize anything."

"When were you built?"

And none of George Price's snappy comebacks came from him.

"Just spending another evening in the bosom of my family.
What are you doing?"

Even as late as the late 1970s, as Michael Maslin's story indicates, *The New Yorker* would buy cartoon ideas from cartoonists and have them redrawn by the established stars, like Whitney Darrow or Charles Addams. This is also how Mick Stevens got his foot in the door, before squeezing the rest of himself through.

There's no doubt that this way of doing things produced some very fine cartoons. By separating the drawing part from the idea part, you got a high level of both. In terms of pure draftmanship, the work of cartoonists like George Price and Peter Arno is unmatched.

Nevertheless, people are often at least a little disappointed, and sometimes more than a little, when they find out that a cartoonist did not come up with an idea but only executed it, no matter how beautifully. It's a question of authenticity, and by the 1970s authenticity had become an important cultural value. You wanted invention and execution in one individual, and if you could have the invention by sacrificing a bit on the execution, that was an acceptable trade-off. Yet if the drawing could not depend on a bravura performance to wow you, it had to have other qualities. Sometimes the gag was so great that it compensated for any artistic awkwardness, but more often those technical limitations helped highlight the peculiar voice and personality of the cartoonist, so that ideas became less generic and more idiosyncratic. Bob Dylan might not have the best voice, but you'd rather hear him sing "Positively 4th Street" than Sinatra.

Gradually, and then almost completely, *The New Yorker* sought this all-in-one singer-songwriter model for its cartoons. There was a practical side to this preference as well, because the editor no longer had to be a matchmaker. However, I don't think the practicality was what motivated Lee. He really wanted not only new cartoonists but also new cartoonists with new outlooks. Those first cartoons by me, Michael, Jack, Mick, and Roz provided both. Later in Lee's tenure he would add the distinctive voices of Michael Crawford,

Danny Shanahan,

and Bruce Eric Kaplan ("BEK"),

"Well, I do have this recurring dream that one day I might see some results."

all of whom I would gratefully inherit when I became cartoon editor. But I was a long way from being cartoon editor back then and really a long way from being an established *New Yorker* cartoonist. Still, after I sold that first cartoon I fantasized that my life would be transformed. I would be a famous cartoonist entitled to all the rights, privileges, and perquisites duly accorded to famous cartoonists.

As if. Look, getting a cartoon published in *The New Yorker* doesn't make you famous or even give you the right to call yourself a *New Yorker* cartoonist. To be a real *New Yorker* cartoonist, to join the ranks of Steig and Steinberg, Addams and Arno, Ziegler and—well, it's hard to think of any other *Z* cartoonists—I'd have to get published, when all was said and done and drawn, more than once, more than ten times, maybe more than a thousand times. And I was a long way from that goal. But to paraphrase the ancient Chinese sage Lao-tzu, the journey of a thousand cartoons begins with a single gag. However, by the end of 1977 I was only three more gags along that journey.

Many of the cartoons I did during my first few years at *The New Yorker* were completely visual—no caption at all.

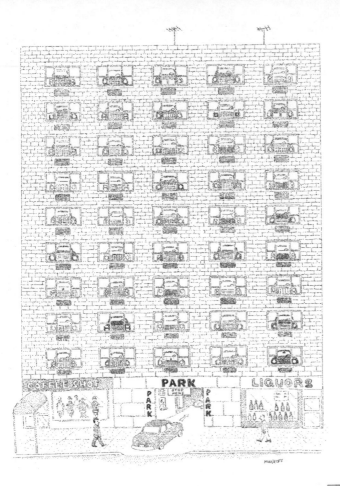

These and others like them, featuring a primarily visual approach, were published a few years later in an early collection of my work.

I had focused on this type of cartoon for two reasons: (1) I thought of it as the purest kind and (2) that's the kind *The New Yorker* was buying.

But I soon realized that by restricting myself to the strictly or primarily visual, I wasn't being true to my own sense of humor, which had always been highly verbal, quick with a quip, a retort, a rant, or a riff. People are funny not only because of what they do but because of what they say when they're doing what they do. Silent film comedy is great, but if we'd never progressed to the talkies we wouldn't have the great films of Preston Sturges, Billy Wilder, or Woody Allen. By excluding speech from my cartoons, I was restricting the range of things my cartoons could talk about. Evidently, this self-imposed restriction created in me a pent-up demand for words as well as images, because when my first *New Yorker* cartoon with words was published, it had a hell of a lot of them.

*"I think you two may hit it off. Craig, here, is an attractive
male academic in his early forties who seeks a warm, vivacious
woman delighting in conversation, arts, and nature for an
evolving romantic commitment, possibly marriage, while you,
Vivian, are a good-looking, intelligent, stimulating woman in
her late thirties who seeks an educated, unattached, well-bred
man concerned with ideas, culture, and the environment with
whom to share your life interests and companionship."*

From then on my approach was eclectic, using words and images in any way I thought would best get the idea across.

"Look, Joel, you're relatively young, have a relatively nice job and a relatively nice wife. There's no reason in the world why you shouldn't be relatively happy."

Three Out of Four Doctors

In 1978, thirteen of my cartoons were published, and the next year I almost doubled that number, including this full-page cartoon, which prefigured where "my generation" was going:

10TH ANNIVERSARY WOODSTOCK REUNION

It also prefigured where I was going as a cartoonist, because you had to be considered an established *New Yorker* cartoonist to warrant a full page in the publication. But to be officially established as a *New Yorker* cartoonist, you also had to have the coveted *New Yorker* cartoonist's "contract," which would be the ultimate stamp of endorsement.

The following year, that endorsement became official when the art editor, Lee Lorenz, wrote this letter to the editor, William Shawn:

December 12, 1980

To Mr. Shawn from Lee Lorenz:

Robert Mankoff has been selling us drawings regularly since 1978. In 1979 we purchased 25 drawings and in 1980 27. He has developed an original and distinctive style and has demonstrated a capacity to produce consistently interesting material. On this basis I recommend we offer him a contract effective January 1, 1981.

The "original and distinctive style" Lee refers to was, of course, my dots. No one had ever created cartoons that way, and no one other than myself has done so since, for good reasons, which I've alluded to and will say more about a little bit later. But its distinctiveness had caught the eye of not only editors but cartoonists as well. One of them, Jack Ziegler, my good friend by that time, created this fanciful drawing of the Mankoff dotorium in his own distinct and original style.

AT THE MANKOFFWORKS

The *New Yorker* valued distinctiveness in both ideas and style—as it still does. Ardent fans of *New Yorker* cartoons don't need to look at the signature on a cartoon to see who's done it, and my dots readily identified me—and, frankly, covered up some of my deficiencies as a draftsman.

My friend Sam Gross classifies cartoonists as either "heads" or "hands." A "head" cartoonist needs a strong idea to have a good cartoon. No idea, no cartoon. It's not that the drawing doesn't matter; it does, but it's a bonus. For a "hand" cartoonist, it's tilted the other way. The drawing is the main show, the raison d'être. Charles Saxon's art—for which the term "art" is completely apt—provides a prime example of this.

*"It's good to know about trees. Just remember nobody
ever made any big money knowing about trees."*

Although I had a unique style that suited me and my work, I was really a "head" cartoonist. And while there was a lot of inking for all those dots, it was the thinking that really mattered. Basically, these two drawings use the same amount of ink, but it's the think that makes the second one a cartoon.

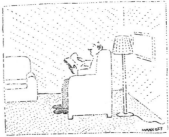

My cartoon thinking at the time swung from the abstractly amusing

to the amusingly amusing.

"Now, this over here, this is why you're going to have to go to jail."

*"And now I'd like to sing a little song written specially
for me called 'I Wanna Be President.'"*

But everything I did, whether it was to be obliquely witty or outright funny, was in the *New Yorker* framework of what I call benign humor, intended to intrigue or amuse but not to offend. It's heavy on the whimsy,

*"If birds fly over the rainbow,
Garber, why, oh, why, can't I?"*

*"The boys in research seem to
think it has something to do
with aerodynamics, Chief."*

light on the ridicule,

*"I don't know, Al. On the one hand, there's no doubt
that it's a make-work, dead-end job, but, on the other
hand, it's also a vice-presidency."*

and the butt of the joke, even when it seems to be the other guy, is usually us.

There's a lot to be said for this kind of humor, and a good amount that has been said against it. I would have to face up to the pros and cons of soft versus edgy jokes once I became cartoon editor, especially under Tina Brown, who was all edge, all the time. But back in 1980, soft appealed to me, and my version of it garnered me the coveted *New Yorker* contract. The next step in my education was to learn what a *New Yorker* contract actually meant.

CHAPTER SEVEN

LAUGHING ALL THE WAY
TO THE CARTOON BANK

Deciphering the meaning of the contract did not require a bevy of lawyers. A good thing, too, because I did not have even one lawyer, much less a bevy at my disposal. Basically, the guts of the contract could fit on this page, and in fact are fitting on this page.

December 15, 1980

Dear Mr. Mankoff:

Confirming the agreement between us providing for the submission of your drawings to The New Yorker on the following terms and conditions:

1. You agree that during the twelve-month period beginning **January 1, 1980,** you will submit to us and give us first refusal (including the right to acquire reproduction rights on our usual conditions, or to refuse the same) of all drawings you make, with the exception of illustrations for the text of stories and drawings for advertisements; and you agree that during said period you will not, with these exceptions, offer or dispose of any drawing by you to anyone else unless you have first submitted it to us and we have refused to acquire the reproduction rights therein; and you further agree that you will make reasonable revisions, as requested by our editors, of any drawing you submit.

2. For any idea drawing we accept from you during the period of this agreement we agree to pay you at not less than your present rate of payment.

3. Any drawing you make which you submit to us and we reject, you shall be free to dispose of elsewhere unless it is part of a series, or uses a character or idea, established in The New Yorker.

4. With respect to idea drawings we accept from you during the period of this agreement we will also pay you quantity bonuses, if and when earned under our bonus plan (for idea drawings) as presently in effect or as hereafter modified or revised, such bonus payments, however, to be made only if and to the extent permissible by law. Bonuses are calculated on payments for idea drawings only. We reserve the right at any time to alter or revise in any manner any or all of the provisions of our quantity bonus plan.

The good part was that I'd be paid more than I was getting as a non-contract cartoonist. The bad part was that payment was determined through a byzantine bonus formula that I still don't understand. The bonus was based on the quantity of cartoons sold (after every ten you got an incremental raise) and on the size of the drawing as it appeared in the magazine, calculated by the square inch. This led to oddball checks for amounts like $331.89, $437.34, and $325.23, which I never questioned then because I was just so happy to be in *The New Yorker,* and because I didn't own either a ruler or a calculator. However, I recently acquired both, and I now think that, over the course of my career, I may have been shortchanged by as much as six dollars.

I wasn't being paid by the "dot," and even though I was a pretty fast dotter, drawing cartoons in this style was an excruciatingly slow way to earn money via the bonus system. Which is why no other cartoonist has caught a case of stippling.

The technique just requires too much time to do your "batch." The batch is the name cartoonists have for the bunch of cartoons they submit every week to the magazine—on the average, about ten. I don't know why it's not called the bunch, but if it were, I guess I'd be wondering why it isn't called the batch.

Nowadays, on Tuesdays, when new cartoonists come into the magazine's offices, I tell them to submit at least ten. They ask me, "Why ten?" and I tell them because in cartooning, as in life, nine out of ten things don't work out.

Anyway, it's better to have more rather than less in your batch, and you don't want your style to limit your output.

But by the time I was breaking into magazine cartooning, opportunities to be a magazine cartoonist were starting to vanish. And in the following years, no style—fast, slow, or even slower, like mine—was going to be a good way to earn lots of money or even the modicum needed to make it a full-time job. It wasn't *The New Yorker*'s fault. Yes, *The New Yorker* rejected nine of our ten submissions, even from "contract" cartoonists, but paragraph 3 of the contract let you submit them elsewhere.

3. Any drawing you make which you submit to us and we reject, you shall be free to dispose of elsewhere unless it is part of a series, or uses a character or idea, established in The New Yorker.

The problem was that "elsewhere" kept shrinking. Magazines where *New Yorker* rejects could turn into accepts, such as *The Saturday Evening Post, Saturday Review,* and *Esquire,* had either disappeared or stopped using cartoons altogether.

By 1990, practically all the other major magazine markets were gone. Basically, in terms of earning a living, it was either sell cartoons to *The New Yorker* or file them away. And even with selling regularly to *The New Yorker,* the living you earned was kind of paltry. In 1990, I sold thirty-four cartoons to *The New Yorker* and earned about thirty thousand dollars, roughly the equivalent of fifty grand today. I don't consider myself crass or materialistic, and certainly not crassly materialistic, but this William Hamilton cartoon resonated:

"Money is life's report card."

This seemed especially true in the late 1980s and early '90s, when the stock market started to boom and the Gordon Gekko mantra "Greed is good" was ringing in everyone's ears. Some of my own *New Yorker* cartoons of those times reflected the zeitgeist that success should be spelled $uccess.

"As far as I'm concerned, they can do what they want with the minimum wage, just as long as they keep their bands off the maximum wage."

"Keep up the good work, Bromley."

"Well, that satisfies our financial requirement."

But the money I was earning from cartoons was not satisfying my financial requirements.

In an effort to boost my income, I even branched out from *The New Yorker* mother ship and signed on with the United Features newspaper syndicate to do a daily financial cartoon called *Dollars and Nonsense.*

Some decent cartoons came out of this

"I don't know a damn thing about monetary policy,
but I know what I like."

"Long-term, I like bonds; intermediate-term, I like equities; and short-term, I like scotch."

and two respectable business collections, but

not enough $uccess for me, because there was now more than just me involved. I was a newly married man. Actually, a newly remarried man.

"Oh, I guess I'll remarry someday. But first I've got to demarry."

Some of my new responsibilities were reflected in my cartoons of the time.

"What d'ya think, Boss?"   "Adorable, Dobson, but
baby pictures will suffice
from now on."

"And on tap I've got Enfamil, Isomil, and Gerber Lite."

I wasn't traveling solo anymore.

In addition to our daughter, Sarah, who was born in 1991, my new wife, Cory Scott Whittier, also had a young son, David, from a previous marriage. So I had simultaneously become a new husband, a dad, and a stepdad, and since Cory also had a dog, Barkley, a step–dog dad as well. I was determined to make this relationship work because not only had my previous marriage failed, but the one previous to that had also. Getting remarried had almost become the norm, with two being the new one, but getting re-remarried still had the whiff of three strikes and you're out about it. I was really hoping to avoid whiffing on my final try. My past cartoons on marriage offered some guidance about what to avoid.

"Look, I can't promise I'll change, but I can promise I'll pretend to change."

"Believe me, Janet, I consider you an important part of our marriage."

"Brad, we've got to talk."

"Women want more these days, Bill—it's not enough just to be a jerk anymore."

In addition to money concerns, I began to nervously imagine a future in which *The New Yorker* was buying cartoons from a new generation of cartoonists but not from me. I think every cartoonist—indeed, everyone who's funny for money—fears that either they'll stop being funny or whoever decides what's funny will think they have. Little did I know that one day I'd be in the whoever role.

Maybe if I did, I would have had less of an entrepreneurial spirit, but if that spirit hadn't moved me then, I wouldn't be where I am now, because I never would have founded the Cartoon Bank, which, in a roundabout way, helped me become cartoon editor.

Let me explain, starting with the Cartoon Bank itself. The basic idea for the Cartoon Bank was quite simple: to do for cartoons what photo stock houses had done for photos—make cartoons available to publishers and the general public for purchase and licensing. My original idea was do that with *New Yorker* cartoons. But *The New Yorker* rejected that idea. That really didn't surprise me. I was just a cartoonist with an idea, and *The New Yorker* was quite comfortable rejecting ideas from cartoonists—it did just that by the hundreds every week. This experience with rejection gave me an idea for Plan B. *The New Yorker* was getting many more cartoons than it could possibly use. No matter how funny your batch was, necessity demanded that most of it be deemed not funny enough. Why not create the Cartoon Bank from all the cartoons *The New Yorker* was rejecting every week? That would amount to thousands every year.

Admittedly, some of those cartoons, mine and others, fell short of great. Hey, when you swing for the fences, sometimes you miss. And sometimes more than sometimes. But, really, most of the cartoons weren't half bad, a quarter bad, or bad at all.

In fact, most of the cartoons rejected by *The New Yorker*, then and now, are quite good. This just makes sense when you do the math. Five hundred cartoons are submitted by our cartoonists to *The New Yorker* each week. But the magazine has room for, on average, only seventeen of them. Did the best cartoonists really produce 483 stinkers? I didn't think so. The Cartoon Bank would help those cartoonists, distribute their work more widely, make more money for them and, yes, I admit it, even more for me, but eventually quite a bit for *The New Yorker* as well.

All it would take was someone who knew a lot about cartoons and something about computers, what they could do, and how to make them do it.

That someone turned out to be me.

Computers had intrigued me going way back to when I was a kid, fascinated with toys such as Robbie the Robot, which in a way was a "thinking machine." Real computers of that era, considered "electronic brains," were behemoths that took up entire rooms.

"I'll be damned. It says, 'Cogito, ergo sum.'"

That's how computers were thought of as late as 1979, when I did this cartoon:

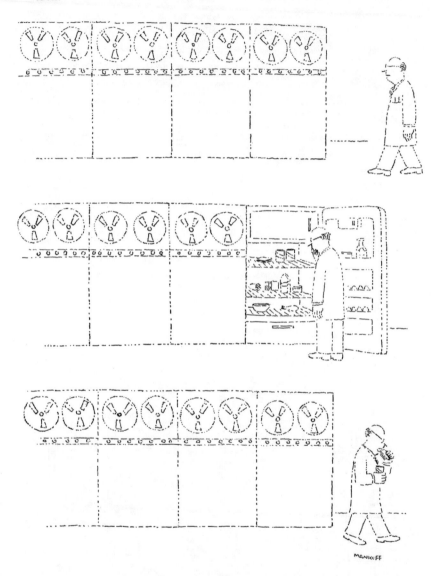

In 1982 I drew the following cartoon for *Saturday Review*, conceiving of Facebook-like functions at a time when Facebook itself was inconceivable. (In fact, Mark Zuckerberg hadn't even been conceived yet.)

*"Fine, Al, and how are you, your charming wife, Joni; your two
wonderful children, Charles and Lisa, ages thirteen and fifteen;
and your delightful German short-haired pointer, Avondale?"*

But it was accurate in one respect. Computers had shrunk, and I had one
of the first shrunken ones, a Radio Shack TRS-80 Model III, on my desk.

By the time I drew this cartoon, for *The New Yorker,* two years later, in
1985,

"All my gadgets are old. I'd like some new gadgets."

my new gadget was the original Mac.

Amazingly, you could draw on it with this thing called a mouse.

In practice, it wasn't so amazing—it was like drawing with a bar of soap, and the cartoons didn't look very good on a dot matrix printer. When I showed them to Lee Lorenz, he wondered what the point was. I had no good answer then, but I liked the Mac so much that I wanted to come up with one.

MacPaint wasn't good for drawing cartoons, but once you had drawn one, it was good for tinkering with it. Now if only you could draw the cartoon on paper and get it into the computer! Trying to stuff them into the disk drive didn't work, but I discovered an early handheld scanner that you would drag across what you wanted to scan. It wasn't wide enough for cartoons; you needed two passes to scan one, and then the software would stitch the image together.

As scanners got better and Macs more powerful, I began storing all my cartoons on the computer. From this it was not much of a leap to think that

I could store all my friends' cartoons, too, and sell them, which is how the idea of the Cartoon Bank was conceived, in 1990—not so coincidentally, at about the same time that my daughter, Sarah, was being conceived.

But the birth of the Cartoon Bank itself, as a real entity, like the birth of Sarah, was not due to me alone. And the same person—my wife, Cory—had everything to do with both. Sarah for obvious reasons, and the Cartoon Bank by completely supporting me as I threw my time and energy and a lot of *our* money in what many thought to be a hairbrained scheme

"Geez, Bob, this is stupid. What have you got, hair for brains?"

and then, in effect, showing me how to run it as a business, because she had experience in running a business—her own, Whittier & Associates, which handled direct mail for nonprofits.

I knew it would take a lot of scanning, because the many thousands of cartoons that had been published in *The New Yorker* represented just the tippy top of the cartoon iceberg. And with such lame metaphors, and many drinks, I convinced most of the magazine's cartoonists that the Cartoon Bank was a good idea.

One cartoonist I was unable to convince was the master gagman Sam Gross, who had drawn many great cartoons, some of which *The New Yorker* had rejected because they were, well, too gross.

Sam was dubious about the whole Cartoon Bank idea, which he called a scheme, making it sound like a scam. He grilled me about it, in his unreconstructed Bronx accent, with questions like "What happens to all my cartoons in the Cartoon Bank if I croak?"

I assured him that they'd be buried along with him, preserving his withered remains much better than formaldehyde. He was not reassured. Even when this article appeared in *New York Magazine,* in 1992,

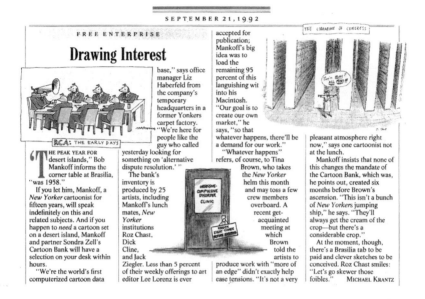

SEPTEMBER 21, 1992

FREE ENTERPRISE

Drawing Interest

RCA: THE EARLY DAYS

"THE PEAK YEAR FOR desert islands," Bob Mankoff informs the corner table at Brasilia, "was 1958."

If you let him, Mankoff, a *New Yorker* cartoonist for fifteen years, will speak indefinitely on this and related subjects. And if you happen to *need* a cartoon set on a desert island, Mankoff and partner Sondra Zell's Cartoon Bank will have a selection on your desk within hours.

"We're the world's first computerized cartoon data base," says office manager Liz Haberfeld from the company's temporary headquarters in a former Yonkers carpet factory. "We're here for people like the guy who called yesterday looking for something on 'alternative dispute resolution.'"

The bank's inventory is produced by 25 artists, including Mankoff's lunch mates, *New Yorker* institutions Roz Chast, Dick Cline, and Jack Ziegler. Less than 5 percent of their weekly offerings to art editor Lee Lorenz is ever

accepted for publication; Mankoff's big idea was to load the remaining 95 percent of this languishing wit into his Macintosh. "Our goal is to create our own market," he says, "so that whatever happens, there'll be a demand for our work."

"Whatever happens" refers, of course, to Tina Brown, who takes the *New Yorker* helm this month and may toss a few crew members overboard. A recent get-acquainted meeting at which Brown told the artists to produce work with "more of an edge" didn't exactly help ease tensions. "It's not a very

pleasant atmosphere right now," says one cartoonist not at the lunch.

Mankoff insists that none of this changes the mandate of the Cartoon Bank, which was, he points out, created six months before Brown's ascension. "This isn't a bunch of *New Yorker*s jumping ship," he says. "They'll always get the cream of the crop—but there's a considerable crop."

At the moment, though, there's a Brasilia tab to be paid and clever sketches to be conceived. Roz Chast smiles: "Let's go skewer those foibles." MICHAEL KRANTZ

Sam, unimpressed, remarked, "Fuhgeddaboudit!"

But five years later, Sam was on board, along with the rest of the magazine's cartoonists. Why? Well, because of Tina Brown, who was mentioned in that article as taking over the helm of *The New Yorker* and perhaps tossing some of its crew members overboard, but luckily not me.

CHAPTER EIGHT

LUCKING OUT, GETTING IN

Abrief digression on luck. There are all kinds, some better than others.

MANKOFF

"Amazing, three failed marriages, scores of disastrous relationships, many financial reversals, and countless physical ailments, but through it all I've always had good luck parking."

Actually, I do have good parking luck. Unfortunately, some of the rest of that caption applied as well. I had been lucky that Lee Lorenz was the cartoon editor and that he was looking for new blood and accepting of new ideas, or I never would have become a *New Yorker* cartoonist—maybe, for that matter, not even a cartoonist, because there weren't other viable markets for the cartoon think pieces I was doing back then.

And I was fortunate that Lee didn't box me in. He let me move away from those kinds of pieces to explore the verbal side of my comic sensibility, so that by the time Tina took over I was churning out one-liner cartoon captions à la Henny Youngman that an updated Henny himself might have been proud of.

I had been selling the magazine about thirty cartoons a year—not bad. But under Tina my sales shot up and I was selling every week—sometimes more than once a week. There was one batch where I actually sold seven cartoons! Why? Basically, Tina went for a joke with a strong punch line. Exactly the opposite of the abstract, intellectual humor of my early career, but my career was no longer early, and I had now embraced my inner gagman, my Queens wise guy.

It was under the reign of Queen Tina that this cartoon of mine was published:

"No, Thursday's out. How about never—is never good for you?"

It's by far the most popular cartoon I've ever done. And its punch line, like Arno's "Back to the old drawing board," became a part of the American vernacular. So much so that it's earned me a spot in *The Yale Book of Quotations*, right there with Thomas Mann and Lord Mansfield.

Quoted in *N.Y. Times*, 29 Nov. 1941. The 1941 newspaper article refers to this only as "someone's comment on Orson Welles," but later writers name Mankiewicz as the source. The quotation is also frequently credited to Winston Churchill, speaking about Stafford Cripps, but the earliest documentation of a Churchill version is dated 1943. *See John Bradford 1*

Robert Mankoff
U.S. cartoonist, 1944–

1 [*Businessman talking into the telephone:*] No, Thursday's out. How about never—is never good for you?
Cartoon caption, New Yorker, 3 May 1993

Mary de la Rivière Manley
English novelist and playwright, 1663–1724

1 No time like the present.
The Lost Lover act 4, sc. 1 (1696)

Thomas Mann
German novelist, 1875–1955

1 A man's dying is more the survivors' affair than his own.
The Magic Mountain ch. 6 (1924) (translation by H. T. Lowe-Porter)

2 What we call mourning for our dead is not so much grief at not being able to call them back as it is grief at not being able to want to do so.
The Magic Mountain ch. 7 (1924) (translation by H. T. Lowe-Porter)

3 Looking back, I imagine I was always writing. Twaddle it was, too. But better far write twaddle or anything, anything, than nothing at all.
Journal, July 1922

4 Risk! Risk anything! Care no more for the opinions of others, for those voices. Do the hardest thing on earth for you. Act for yourself. Face the truth.
Journal, 10 Oct. 1922

5 But then there comes that moment rare
When, for no cause that I can find,
The little voices of the air
Sound above all the sea and wind.
"Voices of the Air" l. 1 (1923)

William Murray, Lord Mansfield
Scottish lawyer and politician, 1705–1793

1 The constitution does not allow reasons of state to influence our judgments: God forbid it should! We must not regard political consequences; however formidable soever they might be: if rebellion was the certain consequence, we are bound to say *"fiat justitia, ruat caelum."*
Rex v. Wilkes (1768). The Latin maxim here, "Let justice be done though the heavens fall," was popularized by Mansfield's usage. *See Ferdinand I 1; William Watson 1*

2 Most of the disputes of the world arise from words.
Morgan v. Jones (1773)

It also earned me the dubious distinction of being quoted—ripped off for T-shirts, decals, and this lovely thong:

But whether ripped off or respected, the popularity and attention of that cartoon cemented my status as something of a golden boy for Tina.

And the attention I was getting for the Cartoon Bank did not escape her notice, either. Two years after that *New York Magazine* article, there was this article in the business section of *The New York Times:*

What High-Tech Cartoonists Do With the Leftovers

By BRYAN MILLER
Published: September 11, 1994

THE company boss is standing in his office, poker-faced, as an employee cringes before him on hands and knees, like a peasant before a king. The employee wimpers: "Corporate raiders, sir . . . one, maybe two companies away."

In another drawing, a man on vacation is lying serenely on the beach, wearing a mile-wide smile as he savors the salt air and sun. An airplane passes overhead towing a banner that reads: CALL YOUR OFFICE.

These and other cartoons that poke fun at the business world have appeared recently on the computer screens of the 41,000 subscribers to Bloomberg Financial Markets, an electronic news service. So far, the cartoons are a hit with the traders and analysts at banks and brokerage houses, where Bloomberg's terminals are fixtures. When the markets calm down, or sour, they tap a few keystrokes and call up some comic relief.

"Our clients just love them," said Elisabeth DeMarse, the director of marketing at Bloomberg. "So far, about 2,000 people a day look at the cartoons."

At a luncheon Tina held for the cartoonists, she told us, including the irascible Sam Gross, that she thought the Cartoon Bank was "a million-dollar idea." All of this was exhilarating but also frightening. Here I was on the cusp of becoming an overnight success at the age of fifty. I had luck and Tina on my side, so what could go wrong? Everything, I feared. What Queen Tina wanted, Queen Tina got, and as long as I was golden, that boded well. Right now, Tina was blowing hot, but she could just as easily blow cold, and then off with your head as well as your headline. Golden boys, under Tina, could turn to lead very quickly.

Besides, my "million-dollar idea" was worth only the equivalent of about six hundred thousand pounds, and I worried that once Tina did the math she wouldn't be so keen on it. Also, whether in pounds or dollars, the Cartoon Bank's revenue was much more potential than actual. Still, by 1997 the Cartoon Bank was up on this newfangled thing called the Internet and was among the first, if not the first, to, in today's jargon, "monetize" cartoons.

THE CARTOON BANK

a division of THE NEW YORKER Magazine

382 WARBURTON AVENUE • HASTINGS-ON-HUDSON, NY 10706

"I gave on the Internet."

©1997 J.P. Rini from The Cartoon Bank. All rights reserved.

Call for Cartoons: 1-800-897-8666

fax: 1-914-478-5604 or email: bob@cartoonbank.com

Button art by James Thurber
©1997 The Cartoon Bank.
All rights reserved.

The Cartoon Bank is a computerized data bank of thousands of classic cartoons - from the most renowned cartoonists of our time. Categorized, indexed, cross-referenced - ready to be retrieved at a moment's notice. We're the world's only stock house of cartoons, a treasury of wit and humor on virtually every subject.

Over 20,000 images currently in stock by more than 50 artists!

Through The Cartoon Bank, you can license for your use first time publication rights, reprint rights, on-line rights - you can even buy the original cartoon if that's what's right for you.

One person who definitely realized the potential of the bank was the deputy editor, Pam McCarthy. Pam had come over to *The New Yorker* with Tina from *Vanity Fair*. At Pam's suggestion Tina had begun urging Si Newhouse, the owner of *The New Yorker*, to buy the Cartoon Bank. The idea was to expand it beyond rejects to include every cartoon that *The New Yorker* had ever published.

The negotiations were carried out with Tom Florio, who was the publisher at the time, and a very challenging person to negotiate with. He was tough, savvy, and kept blowing cigar smoke in my face. Admittedly, very expensive cigar smoke, but still.

First we had to get the minor matter of money out of the way. Once that was settled—they agreed to give me whatever I could find under the cushions of Si Newhouse's couch—I agreed to sell the Cartoon Bank, as long as two other conditions were met: (1) I would continue to be its president and (2) I would also become cartoon editor.

The first condition made complete sense, but the second maybe not. *The New Yorker* already had an excellent cartoon editor, Lee Lorenz, a brilliant cartoonist himself with over a thousand published *New Yorker* cartoons who had been doing the job very well for twenty-four years.

Look, I was very grateful to Lee for having brought me into the magazine, but not so grateful that I didn't want his job. In other words, I was an ingrate. It wasn't that I thought I could do it better, but I did think I could do it differently, by evolving the tradition, bringing in new comic sensibilities, and using the combined positions of president of the Cartoon Bank and cartoon editor to make cartooning more economically viable. So when push came to shove, I guess I did think I could do the job better.

I actually didn't expect them to meet the second condition and I knew they wouldn't, but I felt it couldn't hurt to have my ambitions, both for myself and the expanded nature of the job. And it didn't, because when Lee decided to retire later that year, ambitious, eligible Bob got tapped by Tina for the job.

I'm not sure about how Lee felt about me stepping into his shoes. Probably a bit uncomfortable because he was still in them. Nevertheless, when I took over, he graciously showed me the ropes and, even more graciously, made no attempt to hang me with them. Lee continues to produce wonderful cartoons for the magazine, for which *The New Yorker* and I are truly grateful. And looking back now on what I've accomplished as cartoon editor, as compared to what Lee did in his twenty-four years, I can humbly say, paraphrasing Lloyd Bentsen in his 1988 vice-presidential debate with Dan Quayle, that I knew Lee Lorenz, Lee Lorenz was a friend of mine, and I'm no Lee Lorenz.

Nevertheless, in 1997 I became president of what was now *The New Yorker*'s cartoon bank as well as cartoon editor of *The New Yorker*. On the Cartoon Bank side, Cory came along with me. This could be construed as nepotism, but it wasn't, because by this time she was the COO.

Since then, the Cartoon Bank has gone through many iterations. As I write, this is the latest one, as part of the Condé Nast Collection.

But the basic model is still the same: an online database from which you can buy a print or license a cartoon. And, by the way, as a cartoonist, cartoon editor, and founder of the Cartoon Bank, I strongly urge you do to so. Not for Condé Nast. Condé Nast doesn't need the money, though its accountants will gladly take it; but, as I've pointed out, the cartoonists always do.

An aside before moving on: I'm no longer president of the Cartoon Bank. Why? This cartoon says it best:

"I'll quit when it stops being fun."

The fun stopped for me about ten years into it, when the focus shifted from the Cartoon Bank to using the online platform to promote Condé Nast's photos, covers, and illustrations from other magazines, such as *Vogue, Vanity Fair, Glamour,* and *Golf Digest.* Nothing wrong with doing that from a corporate point of view, but from a personal perspective it was clear that someone who has no interest in fashion, never reads celebrity profiles, is unglamorous, and agrees with Mark Twain that golf is "a good walk spoiled" wouldn't be a good fit to head such an entity.

But back when I became cartoon editor and Cartoon Bank president while still being a cartoonist for the magazine, it was a ton of fun and a heady time for me and, frankly, it went to my head. Especially when an entire *Nightline* special, called "Drawing Laughter," was devoted to my ascension.

Tina praised my cartoons and the creation of the Cartoon Bank. And Ted Koppel celebrated, in Koppelian tones, how I was bringing cartooning into the digital age by using a computer to construct a collage of cartoonists' characters from the 1920s to the present day for *The New Yorker*'s first annual cartoon issue (sixteen followed).

To top it all, Ted signed off at the end of the show magically perched inside the very cover I had created.

I soon learned, however, that not all publicity is good publicity. The *New York Times* article about my promotion started off well enough: "Last week, *The New Yorker* named a cartoon editor for the first time since 1973. The anointed, Robert Mankoff, was chosen because in addition to possessing 'an edgy, contemporary kind of humor, he's a passionate curator of and defender of and promoter of the art of cartooning,' said the magazine's editor, Tina Brown." That article was called "Tradition on Trial as *New Yorker* Rethinks Cartoons." But things sort of went downhill from there.

The article noted that "there is ample criticism of what *The New Yorker* has printed lately" and then gave ample voice to that ample criticism. Examples: Barbara Nichols, a gallery owner who had worked at "the old *New Yorker*," said the cartoons' tone had "lost its sophistication" and "now it's all about trying to titillate people." Peter Kuper, a teacher at the School of Visual Arts, commented, "It's definitely more idea-driven than art-driven." He added, "Personally, I'm always sorry to see the drawing quality go down." And finally Marshall Blonsky, a professor of semiotics (the study of signs) bloviated about a particular *New Yorker* cartoon,

"If I told you the secret of making light, flaky piecrust, it wouldn't be much of a secret anymore, now would it?"

in the following way:

"This is humor and it's supposed to make you smile at the expense of a type. . . . It's making fun of a type that doesn't exist any longer. It's a failure. Young women don't want to make pie crust and their swains don't want to eat pie crust, because it gives you cholesterol." He summed up cartoons like this: "Not only do they not have a shelf life," he said, "they don't have a life."

Fortunately, not many people pay much attention to semioticians, which is, ahem, a good sign. And bloviations notwithstanding, the search for light flaky piecrust goes on unabated.

About 214,000 results (0.35 seconds)

The article's basic complaint was that *New Yorker* cartoons weren't as good as they used to be, because, in summary, they were titillating, badly drawn, out of touch, and ephemeral. My short answer to the complaint that the cartoons weren't as good as they used to be is "They never were." The longer answer will be contained in my forthcoming multivolume treatise, *The Rise and Fall and Rise of the New Yorker Cartoon.* But here's a preview.

OUR LOCAL CORRESPONDENTS

NURSE WOLF

For a dominatrix who sees herself as a healer, can a dungeon be a clinic?

BY PAUL THEROUX

True, when Tina Brown became editor, in 1991, she shook up the staid image of *The New Yorker*—by publishing, for instance, an article about a dominatrix who fancied herself a healer.

Definitely a bit titillating. And some of the cartoons published under Tina were even titillating enough to have actual tits in them.

"This is where they use the body double."

"Must be sweeps month."

"They thought a wire-free party would put everyone at ease."

CASUAL SEX FRIDAYS

Shocking. But, honestly, to be shocked in the 1990s by the cartoon representation of those delightful and universally admired secondary sexual characteristics of women would be even more shocking. As Tina opined in the *New York Times* article, "There's nothing really we don't allow. It's all about whether it's really funny. A big mistake would be to be too prissy. The last thing we want to be is politically correct. I would rather err on the side of offending a few people than to get prissy with the cartoon choice."

Actually, there was plenty that "we" didn't allow, still don't, and still shouldn't, and it took me a while to sort those rules out. But the world of the 1990s, Tina's world, was not the world of the 1950s or even the 1970s, when I'd started cartooning.

Under William Shawn, a glimpse of stocking may not have been looked on as shocking, but pretty much everything else was, especially when it came to sex. Since then, the sexual revolution had indeed happened, and thanks to Tina, it finally made its way to the pages of *The New Yorker*.

Another revolution that the cartoons had to acknowledge was in the news itself. The news cycle was not yet the Internet's relentless twenty-four/seven, but as this 1994 cartoon of mine indicates, it was moving in that direction.

"Many, many news cycles ago . . ."

So we published some cartoons that might appear to have a short shelf life, like Bernie Schoenbaum's drawing depicting a "wire-free" nude party in Washington, which referred to Kenneth Starr's investigation of President Clinton. And these two, by William Hamilton and Bob Weber, directly targeting the White House sex scandal:

"So Zeus was like their President Bill Clinton?"

"Are you decent?"

In the end, all of them would have a continuing afterlife as a comic chronicle of our politics and culture, always available online at cartoonbank.com and in anthologies like *The Complete Cartoons of The New Yorker* (2004). In a *New York Times* review, Janet Maslin called that book "a transfixing study of American mores and manners that happens to incorporate boundless laughs, too." *New Yorker* cartoons had always been timely. It was just that by the 1990s time had sped up, and the cartoons needed to keep pace.

CHAPTER NINE

SEINFELD AND THE CARTOON EPISODE

I didn't take the criticisms in the *New York Times* article to heart. For the most part, people were comparing the cartoons in any given issue with the best, most anthologized cartoons of the past, favorites they remembered and revered. No one recalls cartoons they didn't like.

I'm a big fan of the great cartoons of the past. After all, they were pretty much what went into *The Complete Cartoons of The New Yorker,* which I edited. But I didn't have any trouble finding cartoons from after I became cartoon editor that could hold their own with the classics of yesteryear.

"Scotch and toilet water?"

S.GROSS

"I don't care if she is a tape dispenser. I love her."

CHILDCRAP

"Paper or plastic?"

*"Of course I care about how you imagined I thought you
perceived I wanted you to feel."*

These cartoons are now among the ones people look back on when they
complain that *New Yorker* cartoons aren't as good as they used to be.

They were done by, respectively, Leo Cullum, Sam Gross, Bud
Handelsman, Tom Cheney, and Bruce Eric Kaplan.

Kaplan is both a renowned *New Yorker* cartoonist and an established
sitcom writer, as well as a producer of such shows as *Six Feet Under* and *Girls*.
He's responsible for the famous—or perhaps I should say infamous—
Seinfeld "cartoon episode," in which Elaine is obsessed with a cartoon in
The New Yorker she doesn't "get." The show aired in 1998, not long after I
had become cartoon editor, and my initial reaction to it was "Et tu, Bruce?"
But over time the episode has grown on me, and I realize it's an excellent
way to compare fiction with reality, to explain how the cartoon department
operates and contemplate how humor works without taking too much of
the fun and funny out of it.

To do so, I've created a stripped-down comic-strip version of the episode that includes just the pertinent cartoon parts.

Let's start with the scene in the diner where Elaine is perplexed by the
cartoon.

Elaine is determined to crack the code. So, under the pretext of hiring some *New Yorker* cartoonists to illustrate the J. Peterman catalog, Elaine gets to see the cartoon editor, who has the surname Elinoff. (I wish they had used my name, but I had to settle for the last three letters.) Elaine's real purpose is to make Elinoff admit that the cartoon doesn't make any sense.

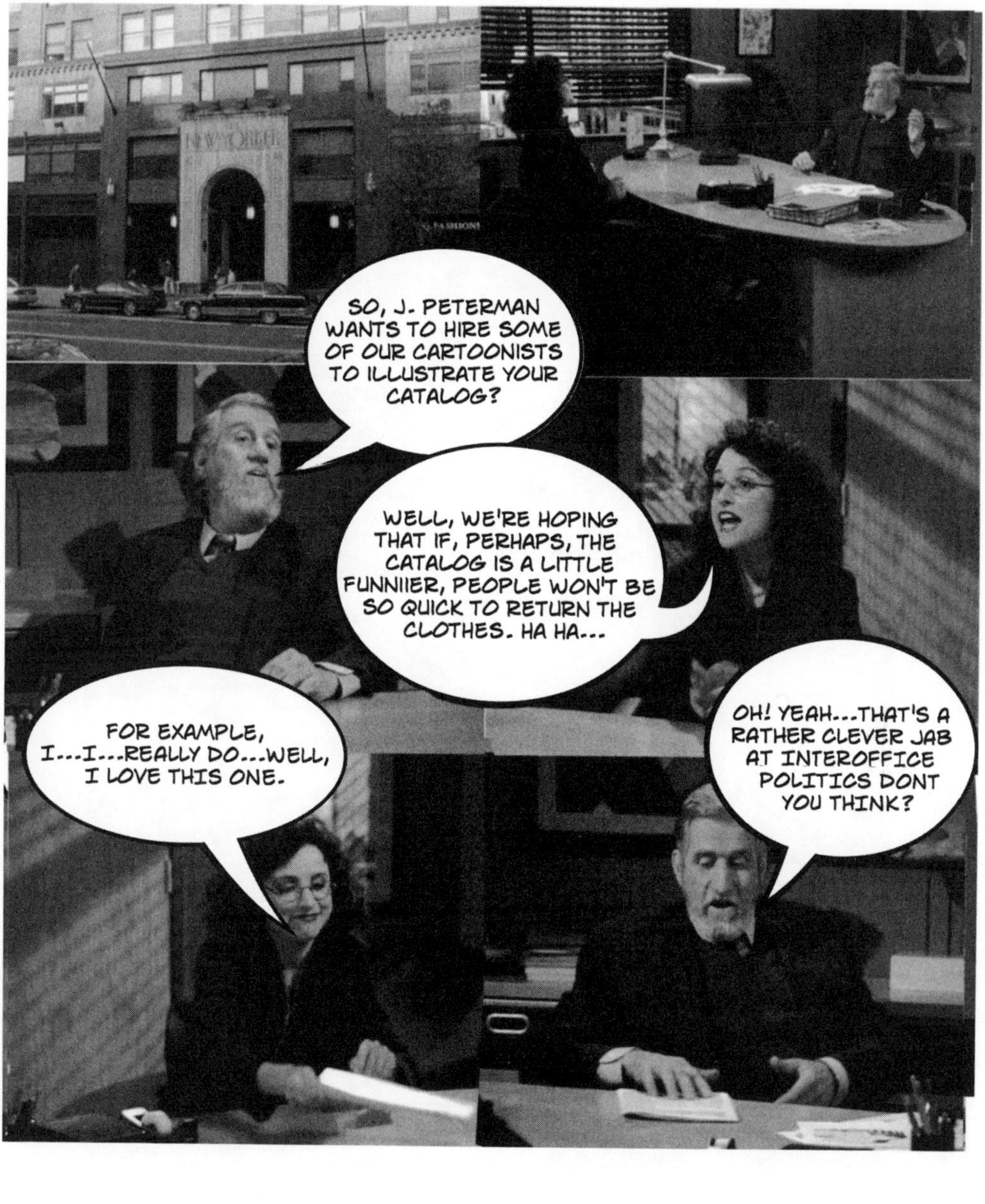
SO, J. PETERMAN WANTS TO HIRE SOME OF OUR CARTOONISTS TO ILLUSTRATE YOUR CATALOG?
WELL, WE'RE HOPING THAT IF, PERHAPS, THE CATALOG IS A LITTLE FUNNIIER, PEOPLE WON'T BE SO QUICK TO RETURN THE CLOTHES. HA HA...
FOR EXAMPLE, I...I...REALLY DO...WELL, I LOVE THIS ONE.
OH! YEAH...THAT'S A RATHER CLEVER JAB AT INTEROFFICE POLITICS DONT YOU THINK?

When Elaine doesn't buy the "gossamer" defense, Elinoff flails about, adding to his claim that the cartoon is "a rather clever jab at interoffice politics" by saying it's "a comment on contemporary mores," "a slice of life,"

and "a pun." There's nothing inherently wrong with these categories. I've used all of them in my own work.

Slice of life:

"Wait a minute—I know there's something we've forgotten to worry about."

Comment on contemporary mores:

"One question: If this is the Information Age, how come nobody knows anything?"

Pun:

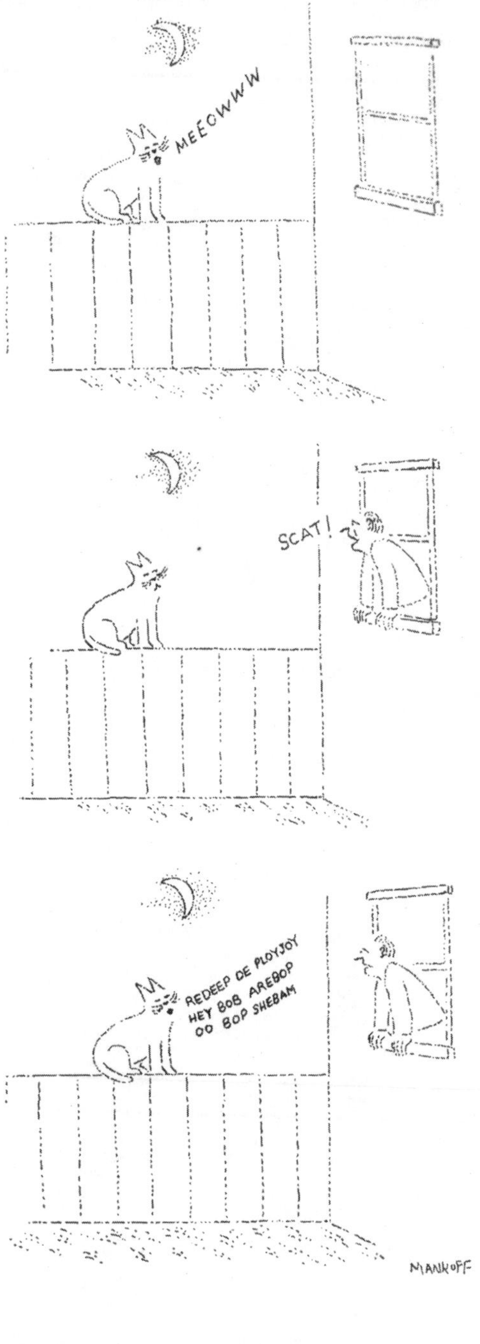
MEEOWWW
SCAT!
REDEEP DE PLOYJOY
HEY BOB AREBOP
OO BOP SHEBAM
MANKOFF

However, these categories don't apply to the fake cartoon in question, and Elaine's withering cross-examination eventually flushes out the editor's real reason for publishing the cartoon.

Hey, we like the kitty, too. Who doesn't? In fact, we've liked the kitty enough to publish not one but two books full of them.

But our kitties aren't just LOL cats trafficking in their cuteness.

They are thinking cats:

who make us think more about ourselves.

"Never, ever, think outside the box."

Still, like the fake *New Yorker* with the fake cartoon in the episode, we do have cartoons with cats and dogs in an office.

"Let's face it: you and this organization have never been a good fit."

"Beg."

The transparency of the humor in these cartoons belies the premise of the *Seinfeld* episode. Even so, the premise is not completely unreasonable. If it were, it wouldn't be funny. Elaine has company in real life. That's why we have run this feature in our annual cartoon issue:

To get the joke of some of these cartoons, you just have to put together the different frames of reference.

"Pi what squared? Long John, you should be able to get this."

In the above case, the frames are high school geometry and stereotypical pirate talk.

> Pirate One: *"Arr, matey, do ye need more treasure?"*
> Pirate Two: *"Arr, I do."*

(And just to be proactive here, I want to apologize in advance for stereotyping pirates. I know that sounds redundant, but in these sensitive times it doesn't hurt to be proactively proactive.)

New Yorker cartoons are not meant to be an IQ test, but they are intelligent humor, which requires a certain amount of cultural literacy to appreciate. So, for example, if your cultural literacy doesn't extend to the baseball sign a catcher gives when he wants the pitcher to walk the batter and the fact that a dog wagging his tail often means he wants to go for a walk, you won't find this cartoon funny.

But that mashing-frames-together method won't work for this cartoon, an early flight of fancy by Roz Chast, from 1980:

For this cartoon, Elinoff's defense

has a certain plausibility, and echoes the famous comment about humor by E. B. White that I quoted in my introduction and bears requoting here: "Analyzing humor is like dissecting a frog. Few people are interested and the frog dies of it."

Many years ago, Max Eastman wrote a book called *Enjoyment of Laughter*, which completely ignored White's advice. Eastman's basic point was that humor is a kind of play, and that if you don't understand that and accept it, you won't enjoy humor.

Play is not the default mode of life; seriousness is. But play is the default mode in cartooning. What cartoonists do is play with incongruities along a continuum stretching from reality-based humor to nonsense, then invite you to play along with them. Where on the continuum the invitation is placed often determines how you RSVP.

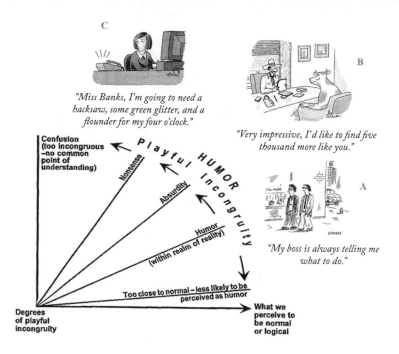

C

"Miss Banks, I'm going to need a hacksaw, some green glitter, and a flounder for my four o'clock."

B

"Very impressive, I'd like to find five thousand more like you."

A

"My boss is always telling me what to do."

Confusion (too incongruous –no common point of understanding)

Playful HUMOR Incongruity

Nonsense

Absurdity

Humor (within realm of reality)

Too close to normal – less likely to be perceived as humor

Degrees of playful incongruity

What we perceive to be normal or logical

In this diagram, A is realistic humor and B is not, but both are completely "gettable," while C isn't. C doesn't produce that jolt you get when you suddenly understand a joke. It's not totally random, though. There is some method to its madness. C uses the classic triplet structure of a joke.

"You're right—things *are* funnier in threes."

The triad is "hacksaw," "green glitter," and "flounder"—three terms you will find together only in one place when you do a Google search, and that place is Harry Bliss's cartoon. So, even though the cartoon is far along on the incongruity dimension, its style of Mad Libs humor is not completely foreign. After all, most people have played Mad Libs. But Roz's cartoon offers no such familiarity and takes many people out of their comic comfort zone:

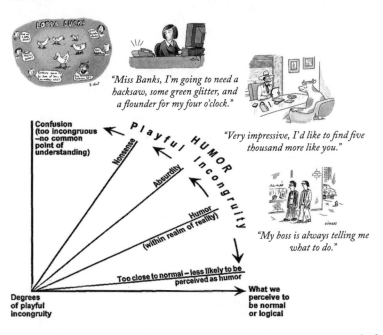

"Miss Banks, I'm going to need a hacksaw, some green glitter, and a flounder for my four o'clock."

"Very impressive, I'd like to find five thousand more like you."

"My boss is always telling me what to do."

Including cartoonists. When Roz's cartoon first came out, it provoked outrage among some cartoonists, who thought its appearance in the magazine sounded the death knell for traditional gag cartooning. Well, gag cartooning is still with us some thirty years later and so, of course, is Roz, who has established her own tradition.

Interestingly, the outrage Elaine expressed at her meeting with Elinoff is directed at classic genre cartoons.

YOU PEOPLE SHOULD BE ASHAMED OF YOURSELVES.

YOU DOODLE A COUPLE OF BEARS AT A COCKTAIL PARTY TALKING ABOUT THE STOCK MARKET, AND YOU THINK YOU'RE DOING COMEDY.

In response to Elaine's criticism, Elinoff responds by complimenting her on the very premise she is deriding.

ACTUALLY, THAT'S NOT BAD.

The flattery quickly causes Elaine to change her tune and proudly proclaim,

REALLY? YOU KNOW I HAVE OTHERS.

Which brings us to the next part of the episode.

WELL, BOYS, I DID IT. I HAD TO STAY UP ALL NIGHT, BUT I FINALLY CAME UP WITH A A GREAT NEW YORKER CARTOON.

PRETTY GOOD.

PRETTY GOOD? THIS IS A GEM!

IT'S A PIG AT A COMPLAINT DEPARTMENT.

AND HE'S SAYING, "I WISH I WAS TALLER." SEE?

When Jerry doesn't accede to the gemlike quality of the cartoon, Elaine presses on, trying to explain its luster. Now it's a role reversal from when Elinoff was attempting to explain the *New Yorker* cartoon to her.

Let's see if she does any better.

At first Elaine goes for the incongruity justification, saying that the pig's complaint is "not normal." That's absolutely true on many levels. First off, pigs are notorious noncomplainers. They may not be as contented as cows, but there is the expression "Happy as a pig in Vorshtein." Ah, got you on that one, didn't I? You were expecting some other word, and "Vorshtein" was surprising and incongruous in that context, just as it was when Elinoff used it as a category of humor.

Most people would agree that humor involves an idea, image, or text that is in some sense incongruous, unusual, unexpected, surprising, or, as Elaine says, "not normal." But "not normal" is not enough even when there is lots of not normalcy, as in Elaine's cartoon. To wit: pigs don't complain, and even if they did it wouldn't be about their height, and even then it wouldn't occur in a department store. So we have incongruity raised to the third power but still no joke.

Incongruity may be a necessary condition for humor, but it's not sufficient. The different frames of reference have to be connected, even if only tangentially.

The Vorshtein gag in the episode is like that. The name Vorshtein sounds crazy but also sounds right. As if it might belong to some eminent Dr. Vorshtein with his eponymous Vorshtein effect, known to explain all that had been previously inexplicable, like humor and Libor rates.

Had Elinoff said "crab cakes" instead of "Vorshtein," it would have been even more incongruous but not funny. Had he said "Koestler," it also wouldn't have been funny but at least the reference would have relevance for humor theorists.

Arthur Koestler, perhaps best known for his anti-totalitarian novel *Darkness at Noon,* also wrote an interesting book called *The Act of Creation,* in which he linked the creative processes behind humor, art, and science. For humor he coined the terms "bisociation" to refer to the mental process involved in perceiving humorous incongruity.

Bisociation is like a mash-up in your mind, when you simultaneously associate an idea or object with two fields ordinarily not regarded as related. The pun is perhaps the simplest form of humorous bisociation, and it's what Jerry uses when he takes a stab at a caption.

That satisfies Koestler's criteria for humor because it brings together two different meanings of "sty" simultaneously. Having a pig as the protagonist in a cartoon lends itself to that punning sort of thing.

"Your constant cries to cut the pork sadden me, Senator."

But now Elaine is the unsatisfied one, and she complains that Jerry's caption is too "jokey." Then, taking another page from Elinoff's playbook, Elaine positions her cartoon as a "slice of life," saying of her caption, "That's nice. That's real." That contradicts her earlier justification of it being not normal, but that doesn't matter. Consistency is the hobgoblin of little minds and the bane of rapid-fire dialogue humor, which *Seinfeld* excels at. That's why Jerry can easily do a 180 from his previous assessment of the cartoon as "Pretty good."

I'm with Jerry on this one. The cartoon does stink. It doesn't make any sense, which makes perfect sense because that is the whole premise of the episode, the alleged inscrutability of *New Yorker* cartoons.

If Elaine had submitted that cartoon to me, I would have advised her to make the cartoon more scrutable by losing the pig and changing the complainer to a shortish guy. And instead of complaints, maybe have the department be called "Adjustments," as though his height could be "adjusted." Not a great cartoon by any means, but at least not the dreaded "woolly."

That is hypothetical, however, and not because Elaine is just a sitcom character but because that's just not the way it's done. In all the years I've been cartoon editor, we've never published a cartoon by someone like Elaine. Why? Simple: she's not a cartoonist. Just as novelists are the people who produce novels, cartoonists are where cartoons come from.

Not that so-called civilians don't pitch me cartoons. That happens to all cartoonists, but being cartoon editor of *The New Yorker*, with the accompanying status that entails, also means that you get pitched by some pretty high-status people—and even an occasional famous novelist or playwright. For instance, one day my assistant told me that Norman Mailer was on the phone and would like to speak to me.

"I'm sure he's got the wrong department," I said. "Probably wants Fiction."

"No, he wants to talk to you about his cartoons. He says he'd like to come in to show you his cartoons."

I agreed. When he arrived, I said, "Really, Mr. Mailer, you do cartoons?"

To which he replied, "I wouldn't call them cartoons, exactly."

Exactly.

Well, at least they weren't a couple of bears talking about the stock market. He later published them in a book called *Modest Gifts*. Let's just say it was a very apt title.

Shortly after I became cartoon editor, David Mamet sent me this note:

I sent a note back to him, thanking him and saying I had taken the liberty of sending him a play.

I know that anecdotes like these make me seem like a snotty smart-ass, and I plead guilty; but—and this won't be news to you by now—I take cartoons very seriously, and I expect the people who draw them to do the same.

I previously made the analogy between *The New Yorker* and the New York Yankees, explaining that getting into *The New Yorker* as a cartoonist is the equivalent of getting signed by the Yankees as a baseball player. So coming into my office and basically saying you'd like to give this cartoon thing a try is like showing up at the stadium requesting a tryout.

This is not to say that only cartoonists can come up with a good idea for a cartoon. As I've mentioned, gag writers used to think up funny ideas that were then drawn by cartoonists. But back then, gag writing itself was a job, like writing for a sitcom is today.

And, yes, even nonprofessionals can think of something funny for Elaine's two bears at the cocktail party to say. That's why we created the cartoon caption contest, to give budding Elaines a way to channel their inner cartoonist. In fact, in the spirit of turnabout is fair play, we took Elaine's setup and used it for one of our caption contests. Of course, hundreds of *Seinfeld* aficionados played along and entered Elaine's caption, but we were actually looking for a good caption, and we found it with this winning entry:

"Stop sending me spam!"

The caption contest is one of the magazine's most popular features. Now, be patient: I'm going to devote an entire chapter to telling you all about it and how to increase your chances of winning (marginally).

However, as popular as the contest is, this type of crowdsourcing is not the way we "toon" *The New Yorker* each week. To start off, we use another crowd—our crowd, *New Yorker* cartoonists.

CHAPTER TEN

TOONING *THE NEW YORKER:* WHERE CARTOONS COME FROM

Each cartoon that ends up in *The New Yorker* starts in the mind of a cartoonist. Cartoonists know that their job is to come up with, on average, ten cartoons each week, more or less but not *too* much less. "Less is more" may be a good motto for some art forms, but cartooning is not one of them. Generally speaking, the more cartoons you submit, the greater the chance that one of them will be selected. To get good ideas in any field, the best method is to generate lots of ideas and throw out the bad ones. Different cartoonists have different ways of getting quality from quantity.

One division is between the doodle firsters and the word firsters. The doodle firsters doodle away until a drawing inspires something funny, while the words first people write, write, and write some more until something clicks.

Jack Ziegler is definitely a doodle firster. Here's his description of the genesis of a cartoon, using this one as an example:

"How are you fixed for oats?"

I'm sitting in a comfortable chair, doodling on a clipboard in search of an idea. I'm on my second or third cup of morning joe. I try not to raise my eyes from the blank sheet of paper on the clipboard because there are too many distractions in the room—and I'm easily distracted. If I allow my eyes to light on any of the spines of any of the books, LPs, or CDs on the shelves that surround me, I'm a goner. Not to mention the pictures on the walls, mostly framed cartoon originals accumulated over the years from friends in the profession. If I look up, I know there'll be one of these pictures that needs straightening, and if I give in to that urge, I'm just asking for that Jesse James moment: the bullet in the back from that dirty little coward who shot Mr. Howard, which would be the biggest distraction of all.

I'm trying to come up with cartoon ideas. I find that if I have nothing written down already—a preconceived idea or setup, say—I generally start my doodling process, my search for something tangible, by drawing a man's head. Sometimes the face will look like there's something going on just out of my eyesight. What is it? I have no idea, but I go ahead and attempt to draw it anyway. Today I'm looking at this guy's head from a three-quarter angle behind him. I give him a cowboy hat, because is there any person more fun to draw than a cowboy? Probably not. I should probably put him on a horse. The horse I've drawn seems to be looking down, so maybe he's high up on a hill that both of them, in their prairie wanderings, have just happened upon. There's obviously something down there in the valley below. I've dressed my cowboy in a jacket that looks vaguely modern. Possibly shearling? Kinda screams Ralph Lauren in a western mojo, doesn't it? It's then just a short, logical hop of the imagination from that jacket to a shopping mall, isn't it? So I draw the mall down there in the valley, surrounded by a lot full of cars. What's the cowboy going to do? Rein his horse off to the right in order to skirt the mall? Or will he succumb to an urge to shop? And if that's the case, shopping for whom? His wife? Girlfriend? Himself? Nope.

For me, an idea for a cartoon generally springs from a tiny germ, which I keep adding to until it builds into something that slowly begins to make a semblance of sense. Sometimes this construction project can be quite elaborate and consume an hour or more but ultimately lead to a dead end. Other times it can take a mere few minutes and get me somewhere worthwhile. Either way, the journey can be fun, and occasionally I find a jackpot at the end.

The cartoonist Matt Diffee's journey, aside from a similar dependence on coffee, takes a different, word-firster route.

I don't doodle. I've got nothing against folks who do, but I've never come up with a decent cartoon idea that way. When I need an idea, which is always, I sit down with a full pot of coffee and a blank sheet of paper and I write. I'll jot down a phrase I've heard or just a single word. It can be something that feels sorta funny to me or not. It's just something to get the process started. Occasionally it'll be words that describe an image or concept—like, I might write down "dog afraid of vacuum cleaner" or "two beavers talking," but I never draw those things until I've actually got a joke idea.

A good example of how this typically works is in this cartoon:

SKYWRITER'S BLOCK

I started by jotting down the words "writer's block." For some reason, these words pop into my head a lot during writing sessions, as do the phrases "I got nothing" and "I should have gone to law school." Anyway, I started by playing with those words. First I thought of alternative meanings of the words themselves. So "writer's block" could be a city block where writers live. It could be writers playing with children's building blocks, or a football block performed by a writer. You can see there's probably a joke to be had among those options, but I don't think it would be a very good one. Might be more "punny" than funny. You could mess around with the "writer" part of the phrase, too, and make it "rider's block." You could take that as far as you wanted and get "horse rider's block" or "subway rider's block." I don't think I pursued that angle very much. I mostly thought in terms of replacing the "writer" with another occupation. I jotted down things like "dentist's block," "taxidermist's block," "proctologist's block," "ventriloquist's block," and then a bunch of occupations that end in "-er," like "plumber's block" and "butcher's block" (which has its own punny potential). In the end, I found the gag by successively adding words to the phrase. Where can you add words to it? In the middle? Not really. At the end? "Writer's block and tackle." "Writer's blockade." At the beginning? Sure, "copywriter's block," "grant writer's block." Then eventually I came to "skywriter's block"—*Bam,* there's the idea. And it came fully intact. I immediately saw the whole image exactly how I ended up drawing it here. That's the best part of doing this for a living: going from the moment when you have no idea at all to the moment when you have an idea. In a way, I think it's the same experience for the reader, except it happens a lot faster. Hopefully.

So that's how I get 90 percent of my ideas. Some come other ways, and I'll take 'em any way I can, but mostly it's this rational, relentless pursuit. Doodling seems like an unnecessary step, and, honestly, my mind-set when I'm drawing isn't really a creative mind-set. It's a mundane-task mind-set, like when I'm folding laundry or doing dishes. Sure, a cartoon can flit into my mind while I'm doing those kinds of tasks, but it's rare and I'm better off doing dishes than doodles, because if it doesn't happen at least I'll have clean dishes. I need that more than I need another stack of Diffee doodles.

Even though Jack and Matt are on different sides of the doodle-first/word-first divide, they are both what I call "cartoon firsters," in that they draw their inspiration more from previous cartoons, their own and others, than from the "real" world. This is the great and enduring cartoon game, in which genres such as cavemen, Ahab and the white whale, and beached whales become cartoon tropes manipulated for their own sake and not as commentary. In this game, each good idea that gets published becomes part of the collective cartoon unconscious. At a certain point, a genre—desert islands, grim reapers, suicidal lemmings, whatever—reaches a critical mass, and there is then enough idea fuel to sustain it indefinitely.

A great advantage of genre cartoons is that when you're doing your batch, you don't have to reinvent the wheel. So, using myself as an example of someone employing this method, here are some cartoons about inventing the wheel.

I first drew (1) two stone wheels, one round and one square. I didn't know where I would go with this, but I knew that it would enable me to start associating them with different frames of reference. I quickly associated the "square" wheel with two things: a bad car, or "clunker," and a prototype of the round wheel.

I melded the square and round wheels together in one structure (2), thereby creating an incongruity—something out of place, odd, or surprising that provokes a tension that needs to be resolved by the caption. I came up with a caption: "The back part I call 'the wheel,' the front part 'the brake.'" Once I wrote that caption, I thought it would also be incongruous if the guy who invented the wheel called it fire (3). Dumb, but I found it funny, and a lot of humor is just playing dumb. This type of mislabeling is actually one of the first ways children make jokes. They call a dog a cat and so on.

I had early on made the association with fire as one of the inventions we think of when we consider the wheel, so I drew a wheel on fire and labeled it a "twofer" invention (4). I knew that joke would need work and figured I'd come back to it later.

In the final joke I imagined the wheel as a car a teenager might want to borrow (5). But that would only be the final joke for this session. Any one of these five jokes could be expanded—maybe not ad infinitum but certainly ad nauseam, so I'll stop for now.

In contrast to the cartoon firsters are what I call the reality firsters. They might start with words or images and can employ the classic genres or not, but the humor in their cartoons relates to the real world, whether events in the news or their own personal lives. The cartooning work ethic doesn't change—these cartoonists also put in a lot of time—but the motivating forces behind the ideas is different. One way to identify someone from this school of cartooning is to ask yourself how much you can infer of the cartoonist's personality and worldview from their cartoons. From Jack and Matt's drawings, I would venture only that they are imaginative and funny.

But the cartoons of someone like Roz Chast are much more revealing. While Roz's early cartoons were in the absurdist mode and let on little about her except that she had a brilliantly idiosyncratic sense of humor,

THE VELCROS AT HOME

as time went by, absurdity converged with anxiety, giving us a window into her alternative universe.

Here's how she converts the troubling into the comical:

> The deadline I have set for myself is Tuesday evening. I generally turn in from five to eight drawings. Some of mine are a full page or even two pages. That still counts as one drawing to me, because it's still one idea.
>
> During the week, I jot cartoon ideas down: conversations I overhear, random things that suddenly seem funny to me, something idiotic I've just done, whatever seems like it could turn into a cartoon. But I don't sit down at my desk to actually work on the batch until Monday. If I work too many days before the deadline, I start worrying and fuss with drawings until I tear them up.
>
> So Monday and Tuesday are my *New Yorker* batch days. I sit at my desk, drawing, writing, and thinking, from (late) morning till evening. Coffee is good. E-mail is not so good. A quiet room, not too hot and not too cold, is very, very good. I like to give myself enough time to work, but not so much that I get overanalytical and start arguments with myself. On those days, I don't make other plans, I don't work on other projects, I don't go out to lunch. I try not to get distracted, so I can give myself over to that frame of mind where maybe something interesting will happen.

David Sipress looks out at the world to connect it with his own inner reality.

> I search for cartoon ideas in a variety of ways, the most deliberative of which is sitting at my desk and thinking—thinking about experiences in the recent past, or the distant past, or perhaps some feeling or thought I'm having at that very moment. Let's say I've been worrying about the day of my annual physical, which is fast approaching; I might try to come with an idea about annual physicals, or doctors, or death, or even one about worrying itself—anxiety is for me perhaps the richest source of ideas:

"Try thinking about something else."

Or let's say I've just read something in the newspaper that angered me. I will search my mind for a way I can take that reaction and use it to make a comment about how I imagine everyone feels about the news item in question, juxtaposing it with an image or a setting that is surprising and unexpected:

"Congratulations, sire—your financial reforms have been successful!"

Now and then I end up with an idea that has absolutely nothing to do with what I started out thinking I was going to make a cartoon about. The best ideas come this way, seemingly without any help from me—they pass through me and on to the drawing pad before I realize what's happening. For example, after a long, frustrating morning of trying to come up with something, anything, about my annual physical, I decided to give up and order lunch—something vegetarian and healthy—so I picked up the Bedouin Café take-out menu, and next thing I knew, I had drawn this cartoon about the Middle East situation right on the menu:

"Why is it we never focus on the things that unite us, like falafel?"

This division between the realists and the fantasists is by no means black-and-white—and, since it's *The New Yorker,* certainly not fifty shades of gray. Reality-based cartoonists occasionally take a vacation in gagland.

And the masters of the gag can use the genres to comment on something more than other cartoons.

"Of course it would be a different story entirely if we could extract crude oil from stem cells."

Regardless of how cartoonists do what they do, a lot gets done. All of which ends up on my desk on Tuesdays and Wednesdays.

CHAPTER ELEVEN

THE CARTOON DEPARTMENT

I look at about five hundred cartoons a week from our regular contributors and the same amount from others who would like to be regular contributors. Eventually I cull the pile down to fifty or so, which I'll take to the Wednesday afternoon cartoon meeting with David Remnick.

There are four major ways we receive cartoon submissions: by hand, mail, e-mail, and fax. Very few arrive by sea these days. The hand deliveries come on Tuesday mornings, and the hands delivering them are the cartoonists'.

Zach Kanin, here, seems reluctant to give his batch up, but with a practiced twist of the wrist I cleverly extract it from his grasp.

Tuesday is open-call day at the Cartoon Department, and on a busy day it can seem more like a cattle call, with cartoonists of all stripes milling about. They're supposed to come in and see me in the order in which they arrive, but since no one ever keeps track, I usually end up shouting, "Next please, even if you're not!"

In dealing with established talent, like the venerable, if sometimes irascible, Sam Gross,

it's more about schmoozing and lending an ear to his complaints—which usually revolve around the sad state of magazine cartooning and/or his prostate, not necessarily in that order—rather than me critiquing his work. Sam has been called "the ultimate gag cartoonist" and has certainly earned that title with his more than twenty-eight thousand drawings, all of which he has meticulously numbered on the back.

S. GROSS
115 East 89th Street
New York, N.Y. 1012

2 8445

I haven't seen all of them; they go way, way back, some to the early 1960s. The one I'm looking at here, originally No. 6193, was probably done in the '80s. But when Sam decides that one of these, as he calls them, "golden oldies" has held up over the years, he brings it in and gives it a new number.

The cartoon in the photo is one such Sam has tweaked to bring it up to date. It shows a prisoner who is being addressed by a military drone. I don't remember what the caption was, but I pointed out to Sam that he needed to draw a better drone because this one looked like a tiny spaceship. Sam brushed my comment off with "If you buy it, I'll draw it better." Well, we didn't and he didn't, but Sam, with over twenty-eight thousand cartoons under his belt, and maybe even more stuffed in his socks and underwear, is not likely to be discouraged by some comparatively youngish punk like me. Sam is completely his own man, doing his cartoons not for me or for *The New Yorker* but for himself. To quote Sam from an interview he gave to *The Comics Journal:*

> I don't do anything for *The New Yorker* because I operate on the premise that Bob Mankoff can be there today and gone tomorrow, and the same with David Remnick. Somebody else could come in and have a totally different outlook, and I will either fit in or not fit in. If I've geared my work toward the people that were there before, I'm basically embedded with these older people and I'm screwed. But I am my own person. You either take me or leave me, simple as that.

But it's not as simple as that with a very new talent, like Liam Walsh.

Nor should it be. He's certainly his own person, but he's not yet sure of what kind of cartoonist that person should be. I'm here to help him find out. Although self-taught, he is quite an accomplished artist. And I see in him a possibility of reviving the purely visual kind of cartoon that was popular in the 1940s and '50s. Here are some examples of his work:

Liam can't take Sam's "take it or leave it" approach because that would leave him without a career as a cartoonist. He's talented, but he needs help. So, for example, when he submits this "rough,"

he's playing off the complaints box cartoon theme we've used in the past but putting it a personal context. I've done that myself.

"Look, I'm not denying the validity of your grievances. I just think they'd be better addressed at home, Helen."

But there was too much going on in Liam's gag, and it was missing a truth factor. I thought that the truth could be found by making this joke not about an absurdist complaint—tuba playing in bed—but about real complaints a woman might have. So I suggested that he change it into an après-sex situation. That would require a younger couple as well as some additional cues in line with what is suitable for *The New Yorker*. We settled on the marginally transparent negligee and grudgingly on the somewhat anachronistic cigarette as being still the clearest shorthand for postcoital sex.

And so it goes on Tuesdays: schmoozing with the old-timers, mentoring the new-timers, and dealing with everyone betwixt and between those extremes who's submitting cartoons, whether in person or over the electronic transom.

I bring to the cartoon meeting with David Remnick the fifty that will eventually be whittled down to the seventeen or so that will make it into the magazine. As we'll find out, David is an excellent whittler.

This means that many very good cartoons don't make it. I've got to be comfortable with that or else find a magazine that can publish five hundred a week. We could squeeze in quite a bit more if we removed all the articles, but that would be a *huge* loss. One I could live with, but still *huge,* and David might object, not to mention a few readers.

So, how do I look at five hundred cartoons and then pick the one in ten that should move on to the next phase? Simple: I have a laugh meter in my office that records my response to each cartoon; this is then transmitted wirelessly to my computer, which ranks them according to proprietary algorithms and spits out the results.

Yeah, I wish, but even if I had one it wouldn't record much, if any, laughter. There are two reasons for this. The first is that evaluating humor is different from enjoying it. When you're comparing one ostensibly funny thing to another supposedly funny thing in an effort to suss out the funniest, the cognitive effort of deciding interferes with the emotional reaction that causes laughter. Let me show you what I mean. Take this survey, in which the alternative captions come from one of our caption contests.

PICK THE FUNNIEST CAPTION

- [ ] Did you see the look on Darwin's face?
- [ ] I don't like the way Adam looks at you.
- [ ] That's what happens when you eat Brazilian.
- [ ] Now you'll probably want a chair.
- [ ] Those Kardashians are hard to swallow.
- [ ] I'm telling you the apple will be tempting enough.
- [ ] It's hot now, but by tomorrow it'll be somewhere near your ankles.
- [ ] All he gave me to work with was a lousy apple.
- [ ] I told you silicone was nondigestible.
- [ ] It's not my fault that my brain is not evolutionarily wired to like that.
- [ ] Please stop asking, honey. If anything, you look too thin.
- [ ] If only I had hands Gladys. If only I had hands.

See what I mean? The comparing and deciding tends to short-circuit the laughter. The other laughter-inhibiting factor is that whether it's you comparing captions or me comparing cartoons, it's being done alone. People rarely laugh out loud when they're alone. Misery may love company, but real merriment requires it.

Okay, now that I have your sympathy, back to my lonely task. Here are the few rules of thumb I rely on. And if they don't work, well, I have other fingers.

RULE 1: Originality is overrated. Familiarity may breed contempt in other areas, but when it comes to cartoons, it breeds contentment. Cartoons are first and foremost entertainment. All entertainment forms have their genres. The movies have comedies, westerns, horror flicks, and film noirs. TV has sitcoms, police procedurals, and soap operas. Even highfalutin poetry has sonnets, couplets, and epics. Within the familiarity of the form, you're free to experiment.

That's how it is with our cartoons. The cultured readership of *The New Yorker* like novelty in their humor, but they like it nestled within the comforting cocoon of familiarity. Our genre cartoons, such as castaways on the desert island,

"I miss the palm tree, also, but at least we can have a refrigerator."

St. Peter at heaven's gate,

"Wait, those weren't lies. That was spin!"

and our old friend the grim reaper provide that foundation.

"Thank goodness you're here—I can't accomplish
anything unless I have a deadline."

Once the familiarity is in place, the cartoon can be evolved, increasing its novelty. The evolution cartoon cliché itself is a good illustration. Here are some snapshots of it as it evolves over a fifty-year span, from 1955 to 2005, becoming progressively more surreal.

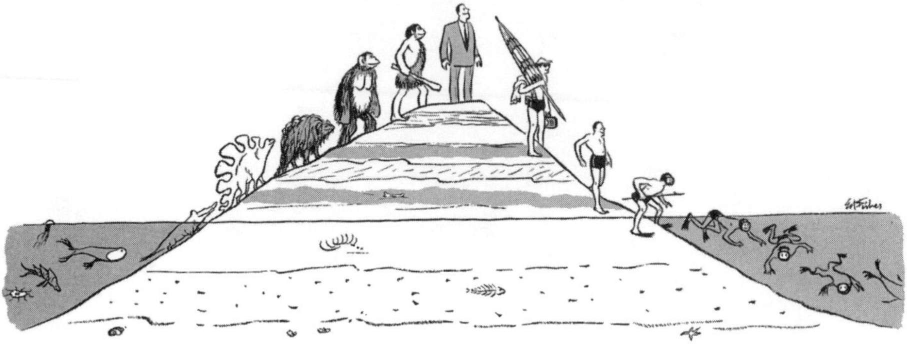

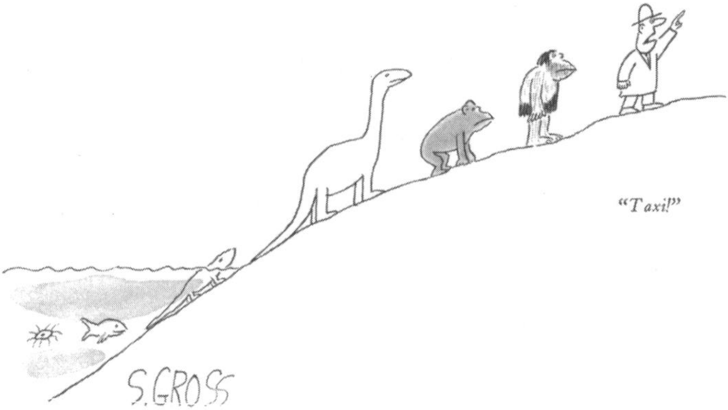
S. GROSS

"Taxi!"

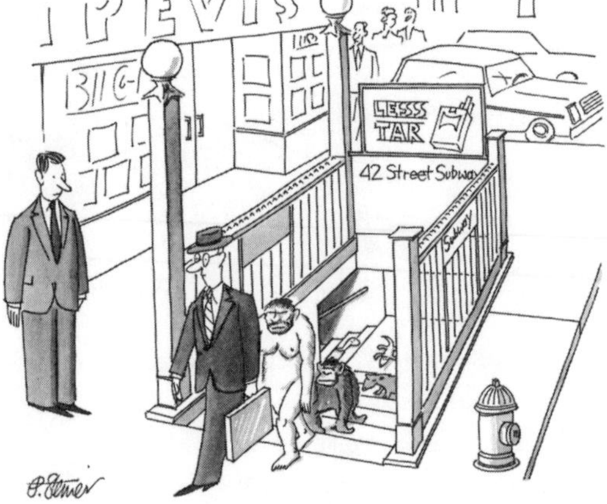
LESSS
TAR
42 Street Subway
Subway

That last one, by Tom Cheney, is way-off-the-charts weird, but it works because of what's gone before it. Speaking of charts, let's go back to one I've used before for the next rule.

RULE 2. Don't compare funny apples with funny oranges or, for God's sake, with funny pears.

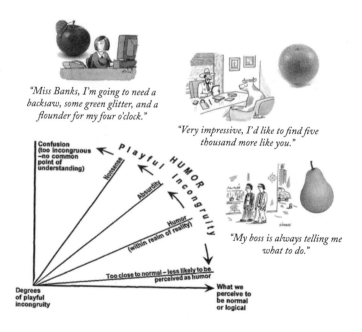

"Miss Banks, I'm going to need a backsaw, some green glitter, and a flounder for my four o'clock."

"Very impressive, I'd like to find five thousand more like you."

"My boss is always telling me what to do."

They're different flavors of funny, and each should be savored for what it is, not what it's not. There's no point in judging cartoons based in reality, that have a point to make, by the same yardstick you use for gag cartoons, whose only point is being funny. "Gettable" gag cartoons, in which the incongruity is made sense of, are a different animal—or, in the above case, fruit—from those whose objective is just enjoyable nonsense. The different flavors of funny are like a smorgasbord of humor, making each one tastier. So, as every waiter exhorts us now, enjoy!

RULE 3. Sorry, it's been done. At this point, we've published more than seventy-eight thousand cartoons. Invariably cartoonists will submit ideas that have been done before or are quite similar to previous ones. Rarely is the idea identical, but that, too, happens.

"Sure it's been done, but not lately."

"Let me through—I'm the victim!"

I did this cartoon in 1993, and a number of cartoonists have, since I've been editor, submitted the same cartoon caption to me. The most recent was from David Sipress.

"Let me through—I'm the victim!"

It's obviously not plagiarism, because it would be pretty dumb to submit a cartoon you *know* has already been done—and by your editor, no less. Most probably David just came up with the same reductio ad absurdum tweak of the well-traveled trope that I did.

"*Let me through! I'm a businessperson!*"

"*Let me through. I'm a lawyer.*"

"*Let me through! I'm a critic.*"

As further proof of this concept, there are times when the same cartoon or very similar cartoons are submitted by different cartoonists during the same week. This just happened last week, with Liam Walsh

"I KNOW WHERE HE IS, NOW I WANNA KNOW WHY."

and Paul Noth.

"Okay. Where is he?"

In this particular instance, it was easy to choose between the two because Paul's was much subtler and, as you know by now, we're a sucker for subtlety.

But there is also the phenomenon of unconscious plagiarism, where you completely forget an idea you've seen and then it pops into your head as your own. Usually, along with the pop a little bell goes off and you have a feeling that it's been done before—but not always.

And finally, I have seen and even experienced unconscious autoplagiarism, where you come up with an idea you have already done, completely forgetting that you have done it. The excuse for all this, if excuse be needed, is that we're cartoonists, not computers, and that's what we need computers for.

But cartoons don't have to be exactly the same for the "It's been done" rule to go into effect. We use our database to check for cartoons that, while not identical, are too similar. This submission, by Michael Crawford in 2013,

"So many wounds, Sam, so little salt."

was much too close to this cartoon of Bill Haefeli's, published in 2009:

"Talk to me. You have wounds. I have salt."

Same for this submission by Mick Stevens,

which came in not long after this one by Joe Dator was published:

"My woman done left me, ran off with my best friend.
Well, my woman done left me, said she ran off with
my best friend. Details are sketchy at this time, so let's
go to Jennifer Diaz standing by in Washington."

RULE 4. Play favorites, as in favorite cartoonists. This is related to the familiarity rule. You're most likely to find something funny if it comes from someone who's been funny before. As soon your favorite comedian appears, you're already put in a good mood that is halfway to a laugh. Our regular cartoonists produce the same effect; it's a conditioning effect, like that used on Pavlov's dog or my poor unfortunate rats.

But there is more to it than this. The cartoons that appear in the magazine are not just a collection of cartoons; they are also a collection of cartoonists, each with his or her own comic voice.

Even if on the same topic, that voice speaks differently when it belongs to Roz Chast,

Jack Ziegler,

Drew Dernavich,

*"When I can't sleep, I find that it sometimes helps
to get up and jot down my anxieties."*

or *moi.*

"I can't sleep. I just got this incredible craving for capital."

And the more familiar we are with each voice, the better we hear what it
has to say.

RULE 5. Don't play favorites so much that no one else gets to play. You can't revere established talent to such a degree that no new talent can get established. But that talent is going to have to show something special to break through. They're going to need to speak with their own voice and not just mimic someone else. For example, we get people submitting Roz Chast knockoffs all the time, as well as those of our other artists. Naturally, I tell them to knock it off.

RULE 6. New news is good news. Timelessness is an excellent quality for a cartoon to have, but in a weekly magazine, especially one competing on Internet time, timeliness is also important. So I'm always looking for a few cartoons to take to David Remnick that are, as they say, "ripped from today's headlines."

"PHYSICISTS FIND ELUSIVE PARTICLE SEEN
AS KEY TO UNIVERSE"

"Always the last place you look!"

"Nice, but as long as there are readers there will be scrolls."

RULE 7. Edit. After all, my title is not "cartoon selector" but "cartoon editor." And although selection is the main thing I do, there is also editing. Most of the time, the editing is rather minor but still important.

The original caption for this Ed Koren cartoon was "Did you procure the worm humanely?"

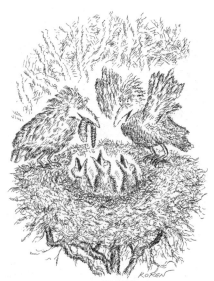

"Wait—did you procure that worm humanely?"

I thought the caption would benefit from more conflict and urgency and suggested to Ed that he make it "Wait—did you procure that worm humanely?" Ed agreed. David Remnick did also, and I hope you're on board as well.

Sometimes editing involves reconceptualizing the idea. Sidney Harris's original caption for this cartoon

was "True, it's been revealed I have a second family, so I've decided to leave politics to spend more time with them." With Sid's okay, I changed it to "True, it's been revealed that I have a second family, but, I assure you, I am a decent second-family man."

Here's a more complicated example. When cartoonist Bob Eckstein originally showed me this drawing, I was a little confused by it.

"Ymf, Y-M-F, ymf."

I eventually deduced that it was a spelling bee for alien kids. But the word "ymf" seemed too short for a spelling bee, even on an alien world. Also, if you have alien words, you can't have ordinary base-ten numbers identifying the contestants. So Bob addressed both issues with this version, which we published:

"Ywhubenqmfpki, Y-W-H-U-B-E-N-Q-M-F-P-K-I, ywhubenqmfpki."

Sometimes I think of a caption that's just not right for my cartoon style or subject matter but perfect for someone else's. In the following instance, cartoonist/fashionista Marisa Acocella Marchetto executed a caption I came up with far better than I ever could have:

"And, in this corner, weighing five pounds
more than she'd like . . ."

Occasionally, and only with the cartoonist's permission, I supply an entirely new caption for a drawing. Michael Maslin's original caption for this cartoon was "I think *mine's* bigger and I'm willing to prove it."

For some reason, probably because I half-remembered this cartoon by Leo Cullum,

*"Take this, Luke. They say it's impossible to get
a decent baguette west of the Pecos."*

I made this visual association between the two images

and came up with the caption "Yours may be bigger, but it's a baguette." I
showed this to Michael and he responded, "An improvement, thanks! The
word 'baguette' made me laugh."

This leads me to the final rule, which may be the most important one
and is the topic for the next chapter.

RULE 8. Make David Remnick laugh.

CHAPTER TWELVE

DAVID DECIDES

The cartoon meeting takes place each Wednesday. David and I sit down in his office along with the managing editor, now Silvia Killingsworth, whose first function at the meeting is inventory management. Each week the fifteen to seventeen cartoons that will be published in the magazine come from a bank of about two hundred previously bought cartoons. Silvia makes sure that the bank is diverse in terms of topics, topicality, cartoonists, and layout sizes.

She, being a young woman, also performs an important second function: providing a different perspective on the cartoons than David or I might have. This is especially true for cartoons about women, where David will often ask her jokingly, "Will the ladies like this?"

And, just by being a third person, she performs a third function: creating a social atmosphere that encourages laughter. As I've said, it's hard to laugh alone, and if it were just David and me at the meeting, he would basically be alone; humor has to involve some surprise, and I can't be surprised by cartoons I've already seen.

At this meeting, it's time to pick the cartoons that will go in the magazine. There is no one better to make this final decision than David. As opposed to my perhaps overly analytic outlook, David's is much more intuitive and quick. It needs to be. He's deciding not only which cartoons will appear in the magazine but also which covers, photos, and, of course, articles. I think the only thing he doesn't personally get involved in is the numbering of the pages.

Overall, David's approach to cartoons is eclectic. He can appreciate a straightforward gag, pure zaniness, or nuanced observational humor. In other words, funny apples and oranges and pears can all make the cut.

I truly believe that once I get to the batch of fifty cartoons for the meeting, the final decisions are somewhat subjective and arbitrary. They are not, however, subject to a lot of arbitration. Every once in a while I'll go to bat for a cartoon I absolutely love but David doesn't, and to settle it we thumb-wrestle—you wouldn't believe how strong that man's thumb is. Remember, though, that when I bring the cartoons to this meeting, I absolutely do at least *like* all of them. Thus I usually don't have a go-to-the-mat feeling for one versus another.

Still, at this point, someone has to believe that there are differences in quality between the cartoons he selects and those he doesn't. This is not a task for a ditherer, and David doesn't dither while doing it. There are three baskets on the table, labeled "Yes," "No," and "Maybe." David picks up each cartoon and reads the caption. If he laughs, it goes into the "Yes" basket. If a bit of observational humor evokes a wry smile of recognition, that drawing will also often get the coveted "Yes" basket designation. A weak, questioning, one-side-of-the-mouth-raised smile—*Is this good enough?*—means a "Maybe" at best. Puzzlement or a frown always earn a "No." Then he reviews the "Maybe" candidates. Sometimes a few of these hopefuls graduate to the "Yes" basket. As for the entries in the "No" basket, well, no really does mean no.

David is able to laugh and smile at cartoons even as he's evaluating them. It's an admirable quality, one I don't possess, but his laugh or smile is a nice validation that after my endless categorizing, analyzing, and theorizing, all the funny hasn't fled the building.

Still, this is definitely a role reversal for me, because now I'm the one pitching the ideas that can get rejected, including—gasp—my own. It's a humbling experience for me, and it usually takes a good fifteen to twenty minutes afterward for my old arrogance to return. Here's one of mine he turned down:

"If these walls could talk, and they knew what was good for them, they would shut the fuck up."

Was? As David has said, "There are certain limits. There's a language limit, a grossness limit, a juvenile limit." And, I might add, a perfectly reasonable limit on the cartoon editor deciding which of his own cartoons get published. In reality, that is not much of an issue anymore. Since becoming editor, I've done fewer and fewer cartoons. Most weeks I don't bring any of my own cartoons to the meeting, because I haven't done any. Why? As I've indicated, cartooning is a full-time job, but it hasn't been my full-time job for some time. I've gone from being a player-coach when I became editor to becoming more of a coach-player now with a lot of new players who need some coaching.

Okay, now that that's out of the way let's get back to the meeting with me, David, and Silvia; it's time to introduce the two hovering sepulchral presences of the legendary past, editors who established what is acceptable for the magazine to publish.

Harold Ross
1925–1951

William Shawn
1952–1987

If David starts to put an inappropriate cartoon in the "Yes" basket, the legends spring into action to prevent it.

Admittedly, that is a bit fanciful, but David instinctively channels Ross and Shawn to determine what's right for *The New Yorker* and also what's wrongety wrong wrong.

That standard has changed over time. For Shawn, any suggestion of real sex was taboo. And, needless to say, unmentionable bodily processes, like the upchucking Chuckles in the above cartoon, remained unmentioned. When Tina was editor, the propriety pendulum swung way in the other direction, eventually veering so far that this cartoon could be published in 1996:

"I just did a huge one in my diaper."

It caused outrage among our readers, and made Shawn and Ross spin so rapidly in their graves that the whirring sound was audible even high atop *The New Yorker* offices in Manhattan.

When David took over, in 1998, he pushed the pendulum back—not all the way to Shawn's era but out of Tina Territory. It didn't happen immediately. We needed a while to shake off Tina's inclination to shock, and we published this cartoon in 1999, which is funny but, as I think David would agree now, not *New Yorker* funny:

"Does this make me your bitch?"

Why? First, because it's gross and *The New Yorker* isn't. And second, because, for many socially aware, empathetic citizens who read *The New Yorker*, it trivializes the problem of prison rape by making it the subject for a joke, which if laughed at would compromise the laughers' status as socially aware empathetic citizens.

Don't get me wrong: I think being socially aware and empathetic is a good thing. But sometimes you can have too much of a good thing.

Our readers can sometimes be so sensitive and so empathetic that they completely misinterpret the meaning of a cartoon. This Barbara Smaller cartoon

"We've found by applying just the tiniest bit of an electric shock, test scores have soared."

provoked such a response:

> I have been a reader of your magazine for years and no longer find the cartoons amusing. But do you really think the cartoon advocating cruelty to children is funny?? Shocking and sad.

This entirely misses the point of the cartoon, which does not advocate shocking children but satirizes, by exaggeration, the cruelty of the current obsession schools have with test scores at the expense of the children's education, and even the children themselves.

An e-mail response to this seemingly completely innocuous cartoon by Chris Weyant shows how important context can be to our readers.

"You may now start packing on the pounds."

Please try to use more sensitivity to placement of cartoons in your feature articles. In "A History of Violence" from July 23, 2012, I found it particularly disturbing in light of the terrible food shortages in the region to have the cartoon about packing on the pounds. Although it deserved a chuckle, in this context it did not.

As these examples, rightly, wrongly, and sometimes ridiculously demonstrate, what's funny is influenced by where it appears. What works in a context where violating taboos is not only expected but demanded, like *The Rejection Collection* (a book of cartoons rejected by *The New Yorker*),

would be wrongety wrong wrong where the expectations and demands are very different.

What David almost immediately understood, and made me quickly understand, is that *New Yorker* cartoons are not just themselves. They appear within serious articles, like the one above, about the financial crisis of 2008—which, now that I think of it, was caused by ass-heads, so maybe that cartoon would work there. But it really couldn't, because one of the quirks of *The New Yorker*'s system is that we never, ever have a cartoon in an article that relates to that article. Besides, that cartoon would still be offensive—certainly to butt-brains.

Still, in setting limits, David also realizes that there needs to be some limit on the limits. He knows we can't stop publishing cartoons like this:

because some butt-brain reacts like this:

> Another joke on old white males. Ha ha. The wit. It's nice, I'm sure,
> to be young and rude but someday you'll be old, unless you drop dead
> as I wish.

> Cordially, B.B.

Or be so sensitive that we can't make fun of our own liberal sensibilities.

"Native Americans!"

*"I hate to admit it, but a man with a big carbon
footprint makes me hot."*

"It runs on its conventional gasoline-powered engine until it senses guilt, at which point it switches over to battery power."

"Something's just not right—our air is clean, our water is pure, we all get plenty of exercise, everything we eat is organic and free-range, and yet nobody lives past thirty."

The fact that David willingly selects cartoons that satirize the pieties of the magazine's readership, as well as the published opinions of its writership, is consistent with his own balanced sense of humor. Simply put, he can take a joke as well as make one. He's quick with a zinger (I know; I have the zing marks to prove it) but doesn't mind being zinged himself. This balanced sense of humor is reflected in cartoons that jab political foes and friends alike.

"This is Lawrence—he does something with right-wing smearing."

"Obama has the potential to get a whole new generation disillusioned."

But their primary targets are the self-centered dissatisfactions of our own well-off, well-educated readers, who have comparatively little to complain about but nevertheless, sometimes, turn that little into a lot.

"Excuse me—I think there's something wrong with this in a tiny way that no one other than me would ever be able to pinpoint."

These kinds of cartoons aren't necessarily the gag funniest, but they are, to me, the most *New Yorker* magazine–ish of all *New Yorker* cartoons. They're not making fun of the less fortunate, and they've not faux rebellious, speaking "truth" to power. Rather, they ridicule their own class—maybe, just maybe, producing some skepticism about its unconsciously held assumptions, and, if not an out-and-out laugh, then at least an out-and-out wry smile of recognition.

For one kind of cartoon, we chuck such nuanced criteria out the window. That's the one we do each week just for you and you, and all the rest of you who, the moment you get your *New Yorker*, rush to the back page, where you see this:

CARTOON CAPTION CONTEST

Each week, we provide a cartoon in need of a caption. You, the reader, submit a caption, we choose three finalists, and you vote for your favorite. Caption submissions for this week's cartoon, by Paul Noth, must be received by Sunday, September 9th. The finalists in the August 27th contest appear below. We will announce the winner, and the finalists in this week's contest, in the September 24th issue. The winner receives a signed print of the cartoon. Any resident of the United States, Canada (except Quebec), Australia, the United Kingdom, or the Republic of Ireland age eighteen or over can enter or vote. To do so, and to read the complete rules, visit newyorker.com/captioncontest.

THE WINNING CAPTION

THE FINALISTS

"I just don't care that much about Medicare anymore."
David S. Goodman, Cleveland Heights, Ohio

"Worst internship ever."
Mike Tringale, Washington, D.C.

"He's pro-afterlife."
Robert Huffman, Stafford, Va.

"I hear he forged his death certificate."
Tom Pierce, Louisville, Ky.

THIS WEEK'S CONTEST

"   "

Caption contest cartoons are also selected at the Wednesday afternoon meeting. Cartoonists submit either specifically for the caption contest or for our regular pages. In the latter case, if we think a cartoon is right for the caption contest but not quite right for the magazine, we remove the caption for the contest. Either way, not just any cartoon image will work.

Here are two basic types of captioned *New Yorker* cartoons. In the first type, the joke is primarily located in the caption, and the image just provides the setting. The boardroom cliché is a good example.

"And, while there's no reason yet to panic, I think it only
prudent that we make preparations to panic."

In the second, there is something unusual about the image that needs to be made sense of by the caption.

"Damn it, Hopkins, didn't you get yesterday's memo?"

In the parlance of humor theory, an incongruity calls for resolution by the right caption. So, for an image like the next one to work as a caption contest, the cartoonist, Drew Dernavich,

had to introduce an incongruous element.

"Shut up, Bob, everyone knows your parrot's a clip-on."

Then the right caption—"Shut up, Bob, everyone knows your parrot's a clip-on"—can glue together the two different frames of reference. So, how do you come up with the right caption and win the contest? All will be revealed in the next chapter.

CHAPTER THIRTEEN

HOW TO "WIN"
THE *NEW YORKER* CARTOON
CAPTION CONTEST

Hey, what's with the quotation marks around "win"? Hey, they're ironic in two senses of the word. First, in the traditional sense of something ironic meaning the opposite of what is said, so partly what I'm going to show you is how to lose the contest; by doing the opposite, you can improve your captions. Second, in the sense of distancing myself from the over-the-top claim I made in the last chapter in order to have you chomping at the bit to read this one. So stop your chomping. Actually, I just found out from Google that it's not chomping, it's champing. Anyway, stop that, too.

But don't be too disappointed. Remember, it's not whether you win or lose but how you play the game (Russian roulette excepted), and I am going to tell you how to play this game better. That will not necessarily make you win, but it will increase your odds and, at the very least, make it more fun for all of you who do the captions and all of us who have to read them.

Now, I don't want to get ahead of myself here. I can't just assume everyone knows all about the *New Yorker* caption contest. So let me slow down, catch up with myself, and get everyone on the same page. By the way, if you're on any other page than this one, please come back.

Okay. How does the contest work? Well, for one thing it doesn't work as it used to, and a good thing, too. For its first six years of existence, from 1999 through 2004, it was a once-a-year affair on the back page of our annual Cartoon Issue. Here's that first one, from November 1999. The winning caption was "Mom, Dad's been on eBay again!" Very 1999.

THE CARTOON CAPTION CONTEST

This drawing, by Jack Ziegler, is just a funny caption short of eliciting the appreciative chuckle that would make it a cartoon. "Mom, Dad forgot the pizza!" is one line that this perturbed porch urchin might be imagined to be uttering. You, surely, can do better. Here's your chance to be a cartoonist—or, at least, half of one—and a shot at being published in *The New Yorker*.

YOUR CAPTION HERE: _____

It took us more than two months to sort through all the thousands of mail and e-mail submissions to select the winner and honorable mentions. And then, in publishing the results, we felt obligated to fill the back page more with our text than the contestants'. Whose contest was this, anyway?

AND THE WINNER IS...

"Mom, Dad's been on eBay again!"

The response to the caption contest we announced last November, in our annual Cartoon Issue, was impressive. By E-mail and by snail mail, by fax and by courier, more than five thousand captions flowed into Contest Headquarters high above midtown Manhattan, where a trained task force fed data into banks of humming computers and crack humor specialists classified, evaluated, cross-referenced, and ranked the entries.

The drawing to which readers were asked to provide a caption is full of specific detail—the huge globe, the rural (or suburban) porch, the apparently angry little girl yelling something to someone in the house—and most, if not necessarily all, of this detail had to be taken into account. This made the task extremely hard—harder than if the drawing had been something more generic and open-ended, such as two guys in a bar or a dog

on a desert island. So why did we go with this particular drawing? Because we (a) liked it and (b) wanted to put it in the magazine and (c) couldn't think of a really good caption for it ourselves. So we figured, Why not let everybody else try?

The "winner"—in distancing quotes because winning is such a vulgar concept when it comes to art, don't you think?—is Vince Banes, of Silver Spring, Maryland, whose caption is under the drawing. (You didn't have to be a rocket scientist to win, but it just so happens that Mr. Banes is one.) He was the first of some six dozen readers who came up with this very same idea, or a nearly identical variation of it, also playing on the eBay joke. So what Mr. Banes actually won was more like a race. Still: good for him.

This caption was not necessarily cleverer, more ingenious, or more imaginative than every single one of the others, but in some hard-to-define way it hit closest to

the bull's-eye. It was topical, depending for its punch on the currency of an Internet fad whose power to get laughs has already begun to fade. But it was generally thought to be quite funny, and it was the one we could most easily see being picked for the magazine in the course of one of our regular Wednesday art meetings. One task-force member—and only one—pointed out that, technically, the guy under the globe should be a U.P.S. delivery man. To this we can only reply, "Yeah, but maybe the dad had it delivered to his office."

We also liked "Atlas Schlepped"—Palma Swirsky's suggestion—but that would have had to run as a title, not a caption. Here are a few more honorable mentions, arranged by category:

ALCOHOL: *"Mom, better make it a double."* (Barbara Evangeline Litke)

ANTI-TRUST: *"Delivery for Mr. Gates!"* (Madhuri Nicola)

BOOKS: *"Mom, looks like Susan Faludi was right."* (Louis Plauché)

DOMESTIC LIFE: *"Heads up, Mom, Dad's adding props to the melodrama."* (Jean Sorensen)

ENVIRONMENTALISM: *"Mom, that Greenpeace man is here again!"* (Richard Viglione)

LANGUAGE: *"Mom! Dad's being literal."* (Pam Inglesby)

LOCAL ALL-NEWS RADIO: *"Mom, do you have twenty-two minutes?"* (Liz Starin)

MALTHUSIANISM: *"Mom, better set six billion more places."* (Julia Sonney)

MEDICATION: *"He's off the Prozac again!"* (Carol Robbins)

MYTHOLOGY-BASED HOMONYMS: *"Yes, he is hatless, but that's not what I said."* (Diane Van Wyck)

OBJECTIVISM: *"Auntie Ayn, your date is here."* (Declan Burke, M.D.)

PSYCHIATRY: *"Mom, Dad's gone bipolar again."* (Maryl Schapiro)

SARCASM: *"Mr. Let's Live in Connecticut and Escape the Stress is home."* (Marvin Ginsburg)

SEX: *"Mom, Dad wants to know if you felt the earth move."* (Mike Gesker)

SHOPPING: *"But I ordered the small stress-relief handball!"* (Michelle Lippman)

SPORTS: *"Hey, Mom, Coach Glick's here to recruit Timmy."* (Paul Snare)

UNDERSTATEMENT: *"Mom, there's some guy here with a briefcase."* (Barbara Schill) ◆

The yearly contest was popular with our readers but had no wider cultural influence. All that changed in 2005, when David Remnick suggested that we make it a weekly feature. What a brilliant idea. I wish I'd thought of it, and as the years pass and memory fades, I'm sure I will have. Still, putting brilliance aside (which is easy to do if it isn't yours), the suggestion staggered the staff because it didn't seem feasible. If the contest appeared on Monday with the deadline for entries being Sunday at midnight, it would be impossible to publish the winner the next Monday. However, it turned out that a staggering suggestion could be neatly handled by a staggered contest system. Accordingly, on the back page of every issue since 2005 have appeared three contests in various stages: a contest to enter, a contest to vote on, and a contest whose winner is being announced. Here is the first iteration of that format from 2005:

CARTOON CAPTION CONTEST

Each week, we provide a cartoon in need of a caption. You, the reader, submit a caption, we choose three finalists, and you vote for your favorite. Caption submissions for this week's cartoon, by David Sipress, must be received by Sunday, May 22nd. Finalists in the May 9th contest appear below; go online to vote. We will announce the winner, along with the finalists in this week's contest, in the June 6th issue. The winner will be given a signed print of the cartoon. Any U.S. resident age eighteen or over can enter or vote. To do so, and to read the complete rules, visit www.newyorker.com/captioncontest.

WINNING CAPTION

"More important, however, is what I learned about myself."
Roy Futterman, New York City.

THE FINALISTS

"This better be good. That floor was waxed last night!"
Preston MacDougall, Murfreesboro, Tenn.

"Would it kill you to use a few of your roaming minutes?"
Jennifer Cain, Brooklyn, N.Y.

"Neither the time nor the place, Doug!"
Miriam Steinberg, Cambridge, Mass.

THIS WEEK'S CONTEST

SIPRESS

Since then there have been more than four hundred reiterations and more than two million entries. And I only expect the contest's popularity to grow now that it's available on phones and tablets. But I'll be the first to admit that the whole toaster-oven initiative was ill-conceived.

That fiasco notwithstanding, the contest has become part of the cultural landscape. It's been ripped off

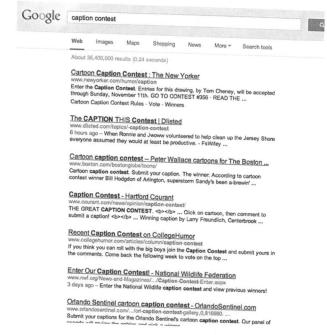

and riffed on.

"Why girls from Stockholm be so fresh?????!!!!"

There's even been an anti–caption contest, started by writer Daniel Radosh, where the goal is to come up with a caption that, as Radosh puts it, "is not just unfunny, but so aggressively unfunny as to make you cringe." Example:

*"Don't make a sound. You mustn't let the others know I'm asking you this.
By any chance do you know anything about gyroscopic inertial guidance systems?
Just nod once for 'yes' and then point to it."*

Okay, I'm cringing. Definitely funny in its own way, but I prefer our way and our caption for this image, which was "I'm not a rocket scientist, I'm a brain surgeon."

The above are all ingenious examples of meta-humor. The primary joke in all of them is that there is no real joke. The secondary joke is making fun of humor itself and *New Yorker* cartoon humor in particular. I have no problem with that either, really, honestly, sincerely, he said, protesting too much. But meta isn't necessarily betta, so let's get back to the real thing.

From soup to nuts, the cartoon caption contest is a five-week process that begins when a cartoon first appears on the back page of the magazine, challenging readers to caption it and driving many of them nuts in the process. This frustration was nicely captured in an episode of *Bored to Death* where George, the character played by Ted Danson, struggles to win the contest.

Jonathan Ames, the creator of *Bored to Death*, said, "I wrote it into the show because I've failed at the caption contest myself a number of times." He's not alone among stymied stars, as a *Wall Street Journal* article entitled, ahem, "How About Never—Is Never Good for You? Celebrities Struggle to Write Winning Captions" indicates. Indeed, the contest has become infamous for frustrating famous people, from Mayor Michael Bloomberg, who confessed that no matter how hard he works at it, nothing comes to mind, to Maureen Dowd, who said she gave up after trying it every week for a year, to Zach Galifianakis, who was so miffed after being rejected that he refused to comment for the *Journal* article. Recently Stephen Colbert, in mock pique, said, "I try hard not to read the *New Yorker* because I never win their cartoon caption contest."

So, what's stopping all of them from winning? Actually, *who's* stopping them would be more like it. First there's this fellow, my assistant, Marc Philippe Eskenazi, known as Marc Philippe Eskenaz for short. He's the first line of defense against the onslaught of the thousands of captions that come in each week.

His job is to go through every single one of them,

which is exhausting. But at this point he can do it in his sleep, and often does.

We make it easier on him by supplying periodic LOLCat breaks to revive him.

As well as a computer program to weed out captions that are too long or too common.

After that, we rely on his own sense of humor, which he has honed at *The Harvard Lampoon* and by doing stand-up gigs around New York,

to make a short list of fifty or so of the best captions, broken down into categories representing the different comic themes each contest evokes.

Politicians in Heaven??

Who left the gate open?
Believe me, he's no angel.
We humor him. He's the only politician that ever got in here.
"Peter, you accidentally let one in again!"

Topical References

It's the afterlife, stupid.
I hear he forged his death certificate.
"And he STILL hasn't released his tax returns."
Does he support the rights of gay angels to marry?
I just don't care that much about Medicare anymore.

Bad Candidate

Exact same speech that he gave 10,000 years ago!
I heard that most of his money is in off-heaven accounts.
"I'm sorry, but that guy couldn't warm up a crowd even in the other place."

Politics As Usual

"If that guy wins I'm moving to Cloud Eight."
Who does he think is going to pay for all that?

Geez he's preachy
"Think he'll get the religious vote?"
"Why bother? The outcome is preordained."
Drudge says he was an atheist in college.
Bad idea. The last angel who challenged the incumbent got redistricted.
Just listen to how he's demonizing his opponent.
I wish he would just keep religion out of politics for once.

Puns, Wordplay, and Cliché Manipulation

He's pro-afterlife.
"I hate living in a wing state."
"Ironically, he's pro-life."
He had me at halo.

Empty Promises

If elected, there shall be TWO days of rest!
I wish I had a dollar for every election-year promise to bring beer to heaven.
"It's always about manna, never about how to pay for it."
He's always promising to turn us into the next Cloud Nine.

Policy Platforms

And I thought immigration was a hot issue on earth.
"Why would we want jobs? We like being unemployed."

With that, Marc's work is done. He can now return to perfecting his stand-up routine or continue on his quest for the ideal caption contest theme song.

Next up in the selection process is *moi*. I aim to select three good captions that will be competitive with one another when it comes time for the public to vote. Experience has taught me that, licensed humorist though I am, when I tried to do this just by myself I wasn't very good at it and was, in fact, in danger of getting my license revoked.

I've had better success by picking about ten captions I like best and then sending a survey to *New Yorker* editors and staff members to see which three they like best.

Please rate the following captions.

	unfunny	somewhat funny	funny
He's pro-afterlife.	○	○	○
Why would we want jobs? We like being unemployed.	○	○	○
I hate living in a wing state.	○	○	○
He had me at halo.	○	○	○
Believe me, he's no angel.	○	○	○
Who left the gate open?	○	○	○
Bad idea. The last angel who challenged the incumbent got redistricted.	○	○	○
I hear he forged his death certificate.	○	○	○
I just don't care that much about Medicare anymore.	○	○	○

With this method, I often get what I'm looking for: an equable distribution of the voting in the actual contest.

THE FINALISTS

"I just don't care that much about Medicare anymore."
David S. Goodman, Cleveland Heights, Ohio

34.2%

"He's pro-afterlife."
Robert Huffman, Stafford, Va.

30.9%

"I hear he forged his death certificate."
Tom Pierce, Louisville, Ky.

34.7%

Were these actually the three best captions from this contest? Probably not, if yours wasn't selected. But at least you now know the madness behind the method.

Let's move on to the methods you can use—mad, sane, or a combo of the two—to increase your chances of winning.

Okay, first we'll go wonky, rational, statistical on this. Obviously, like they say about the lottery, "You've got to be in it to win it." You can't get selected if you don't enter.

Furthermore, entering more often does help. It's simple math, provided that you think this equation is simple:

$$X=1-(4999/5000)^N$$

Where X = your odds of winning at least once and N = the number of entries. (There are, on average, five thousand entries per contest.)

This chart will make it clearer, or at least marginally less wonky:

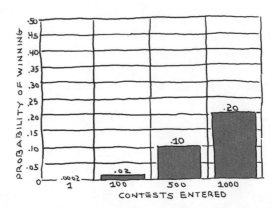

Incidentally, that five hundredth contest will occur in 2015, and the thousandth in 2026. Even at that late date, your odds of winning a single contest have increased to only 20 percent, assuming you've entered all one thousand contests. And your odds don't become even until the 3370th contest, in 2076, provided you have remained incredibly persistent and, of course, alive.

By the way, contrary to conventional wisdom, your odds will also be better if you're a woman. While some sociological research, using college students as subjects, showed that men were marginally better at generating funny captions than women, our contest swings in the other direction. Yes, guys do enter more frequently; 84 percent of all entrants are men. But only 77 percent of the winners are. For women, the figures are 16 and 23 percent.

While entering more often would help in an actual lottery, this is actually not a lottery, where everyone who enters has an equal chance, because in this contest all the captions are not equally funny. In fact, most of them are not funny at all. Here's a random sample of ten entries from contest No. 281:

1. This definitely isn't the quickest way from A to B.
2. Do you have the keys?
3. These Super Walmarts are getting to become a bit ridiculous.
4. Next time just pay the three bucks to the valet.
5. I told you we didn't park here.
6. Think we're "f-ing" lost?
7. I told you—we were in A, for "Amusing."
8. Do we even own a car?
9. That word I'm thinking of—starts with *F* and ends with "you."

10. So, Mr. Time Traveler, it looks like the future isn't what it used to be.

Nos. 1, 2, 3, 5, 8, and 10 are just plain bad—what, around the office, we affectionately call "craptions." No. 7 is self-referential, so also no good. No. 4 is okay but was submitted by hundreds of entrants so therefore gets downgraded. No. 6 and 9 expressed the same basic idea that the winning captions did but didn't express it as well.

"I'm not going to say the word I'm thinking of."

Interestingly, the late Roger Ebert, the famous film critic, submitted the winning caption for this contest. He's the only celebrity ever to have won the contest. Is that because he's funnier than Maureen Dowd, Zach Galifianakis, or Jonathan Ames? Probably not—he was just more persistent. While Maureen Dowd claimed in that *Wall Street Journal* article to have entered practically every week for a year, our database indicates that she entered only three times. Jon Ames? Also just three. And Galifianakis, a measly two.

Ebert, on the other hand, won on his 107th try. He didn't win again, though he entered every week right up to the week before he passed away. Had he lived, I would have laid even money that he would eventually win again. Why? Not because of the statistics of entering more—that's marginal—but because there's a nonstatistical benefit to entering more. Simply put, the more you do something, provided you have some talent for that something, the better you get at it. In 2009, the creativity researcher Keith Sawyer interviewed a number of caption contest winners and found that not only did they enter a lot of contests but they usually generated lots of captions for each contest, from which they selected the best. Quantity doesn't necessarily result in quality, but it does more often than paucity does. It's the Malcolm Gladwell ten-thousand-hours thing, although if you've spent ten thousand hours on our caption contest, you might want to reevaluate your priorities.

The caption contest Ebert won attracted a lot of attention, including the notice of Peter McGraw, a consumer psychologist who teaches at the University of Colorado Boulder, and Phil Fernbach, a Brown University cognitive scientist. They set out to crack the code underlying our caption contest by analyzing all 5,971 submissions to caption contest No. 281. They concluded that we favor captions that are short, novel, don't restate what is already in the image, and don't use too much punctuation, especially exclamation points.

I agreed that long-winded, hackneyed, redundant, overpunctuated captions have little appeal and that shouting a joke doesn't make it any funnier, except to someone hard of hearing. Still, these are reasonable guidelines, and they will help you avoid terrible captions like this one:

> When we reached D and we ran out of gas, you said, "Don't worry." When we reached E, you said, "Don't worry." What do you have to say for yourself at F? And keep it clean!

One thing I will grant that caption is that it is novel. But, as I've mentioned before, novelty in humor is overrated. The humor we like best hits the sweet spot between familiarity and originality, gratifying us because when we hear the punch line, we say, "Why didn't I think of that?"

Like in contest No. 147:

Here is the setup, followed by blanks representing the three-word punch line.

"Objection, Your Honor! _____ _____ _____."

Can you guess it? Right there on the tip of your tongue, isn't it: "Alleged killer whale." Why didn't you think of that? Actually, many basically did, with the variants such as:

"Objection, Your Honor! The prosecution must refer to my client as the alleged killer whale!"

"Objection, Your Honor—the prosecuting attorney should refer to my client as an 'alleged killer whale.'"

"Objection, Your Honor. My client is an 'alleged' killer whale."

The winner, on the other hand, used just the right number of words to make the joke but not one word more. Also, for this contest, the attorney's exclamation point is completely apt.

Satisfied now that you can go win this thing? I doubt it. All I've told you, while valid enough as far as it goes, doesn't go far enough. With these rules, you're in the ballpark but not anywhere near home plate. They're more about what not to do than what to do, so here, at last, is my to-do list.

Shanahan

1. VERBALIZE. Quality of captions emerges from quantity of captions. Look at the picture and say or write down all the words or phrases that pop into your mind, without censoring them, and then free-associate to those words and phrases. Here's my stream of consciousness on this: duck, goose, honk, Donald Duck, the Donald, duck soup, avoid, evade, chicken, coward, Chicken Little, chicken big, eggs, chicken and egg, free-range chicken, chicken crosses road, chicks, pets, petting, sex, children, marriage, mixed marriage, birds, birdbrain, birds of a feather, feather in your cap, bird flu, bird flew, cock a doodle do, cock a doodle don't, cock crow, morning, migrate, migraine.

From these associations, it will be fairly easy to come up with some captions. For instance: "Whoa, Chicken Little all grown up." "I liked you better when you weren't free-range." "I'll bet you say that to all the chicks." "I bet you think you're going to crow about this in the morning." "But how will we raise the children?" "Who you callin' chicken?" "Okay, now get the hell back across the road." "Not tonight, I have a migraine headache." "For the last time, we are not birds of a feather." "Just so you know, my safe word is 'quack.'" "I didn't say 'quick,' I said 'quack.'" "Quack means quack." "Look, I told you I don't care about the sky falling as long as the earth moves." "What if the Donald finds out?"

2. CONCEPTUALIZE. Take a break from the word play to play with ideas, generating alternate scenarios to explain the image or what the conflict is. For this image, a pretty obvious one would be that these are not in fact a duck and a chicken but people in duck and chicken costumes. That idea could lead to these captions:

"This is fun, but we're going to be late for the Halloween party."
"This isn't working for me. I'll get my hen costume."
"Wouldn't it be easier to have sex if we got out of these costumes?"

The conflict could involve sexual orientation:

"It's not you—I'm gay."

Or religion:

"Wait, are you kosher?"

Or politics:

"Yes! I don't care what the Republicans think."

This technique is harder to do than verbalization, but it has the advantage of avoiding the most obvious captions and also of waking Marc up.

3. TOPICALIZE. If possible, we like to pick at least one finalist whose caption relates to something in the news. When this contest came out, in June 2006, the deadly avian flu virus, also known as bird flu, was very much in the news and also in our contest entries.

"Not so fast. What kind of protection do you have against the bird flu?"

"Wait. We really should use protection. You know the dangers of bird flu."

"Please wear a condom, I don't want to get the bird flu."

"Wait, before we go any further: You have been inoculated for bird flu, haven't you?"

"I know this is awkward, but have you been tested for bird flu?"

"Sorry, but I can't tonight—I think I'm coming down with the bird flu."

"I'm sorry, but until you get the bird-flu blood test, this just can't go any further."

"I have to ask . . . have you been tested recently for bird flu?"

"Are you sure you've been tested for bird flu?"

"Have you been tested for bird flu?"

"Do you know your bird flu status?"

"Wait!!! When were you last tested for bird flu . . ."

"Are you using protection? I don't want the bird flu."

"I know you don't have bird flu . . . but I still want you to use a condom."

"Can we catch the bird flu from this?"

"Not tonight, I have bird flu."

"You know, I'd love to kiss you, but with this bird flu thing . . ."

"Bird flu or not, let's throw caution to the winds . . ."

"Wait! Are you sure you have been tested for the bird flu?"

"Not tonight . . . I have the bird flu."

"Wait! . . . before this goes any further I need to know . . . have you had your bird flu vaccination yet?"

"Don't kiss me, I have the bird flu."

"Oh please, Featherly Father, don't let him have the bird flu."

"Um, have you been tested for bird flu?"

"I'm not sure this is the best thing to be doing during bird flu season."

I wanted to pick something from this group, and if they were funnier, I would have.

4. SOCIALIZE. Try your captions out on your friends and see which get the best reaction. If you've got funny friends, this will help. Also, accept their help if they make suggestions that improve the captions. This is not cheating. It's competing.

5. FANTASIZE. Imagine you have won the contest.

THE WINNING CAPTION

"Your Caption Here!"

Also the lottery and a MacArthur genius grant. It won't make any of these more likely to happen, but after all the hard work you'll have put in, you deserve it.

CHAPTER FOURTEEN

THE KIDS ARE ALL RIGHT

When Lee Lorenz, my predecessor, became cartoon editor in 1973 he inherited from his predecessor, Jim Geraghty, a great bunch of cartoonists. To name not a few, but by no means all: Whitney Darrow Jr., Charles Saxon, Charles Barsotti, Frank Modell, Donald Reilly, Dana Fradon, Bud Handelsman, Ed Fisher, George Booth, James Stevenson, George Price, Stan Hunt, Henry Martin, Barney Tobey, Warren Miller, Robert Weber, Sam Gross, William Hamilton, Ed Frascino, Ed Koren, and, of course, Charles Addams. By the time he retired as cartoon editor, in 1997, many of them were no longer cartooning or were being grilled by Saint Peter for all the cartoons they had done about him.

"Coming from __you__, that really means something."

However, he didn't leave me a decimated cartoon staff, because in the intervening years he'd added Arnie Levin, Bernie Schoenbaum, Jack Ziegler (1974), Gahan Wilson (1976), Leo Cullum and me (1977), Roz Chast, Michael Maslin, and Tom Cheney (1978), Mick Stevens (1979), Mike Twohy (1980), Peter Steiner (1982), Dick Cline (1983), John O'Brien (1987), Danny Shanahan (1988), Liza Donnelly, Victoria Roberts, and Glen Baxter (1989), Bruce Eric Kaplan (1991), Frank Cotham (1993), P. C. Vey (1993), and Barbara Smaller (1996).

So when I took over I had, what with Lee's additions (including Lee himself) and the ones who were still active from Geraghty's time, a full staff of veteran cartoonists. All of them had been cartooning for a number of years, and some for a number of decades.

They were professionals, the best in the business, capable of turning in between ten and fifteen cartoons a week, week after week, despite the necessity of having most of them rejected. Sometimes a cartoonist would go weeks or even months at a time, *New Yorker* contract notwithstanding, without selling. Regardless, no one said anything. It was truly a "don't ask, don't tell" policy; you didn't ask why you weren't selling, and they wouldn't tell you.

One time, the cartoonist Mick Stevens broke the "don't ask, don't tell" rule and asked Lee Lorenz why he hadn't sold in months. Lee's answer was

"It's hard to sell to *The New Yorker*." Peter Steiner, who created this classic cartoon, one of the most cited, reprinted, and well known in *New Yorker* cartoon history, tried for years to get a drawing into the magazine. At one point, he wrote a letter to Lee asking what was wrong with his cartoons. Lee sent a handwritten note saying Peter's characters were too ... but Peter couldn't make out the last word. Years later, after finally breaking in, Peter found out that the word was "broad."

"On the Internet, nobody knows you're a dog."

That was the omertà cartoon code of silence that the crowd I inherited bought into. I bought into it, too, because I had been part of that crowd for twenty years. Also, I knew there was an upside to all that rejection, whether you were just breaking in or already established. It kept pushing you to get better even after you had become good. Jack Ziegler, who to date has published more than fourteen hundred cartoons in the magazine and has done more than eighteen thousand, once told me he really didn't feel he had the hang of it until he had finished about three thousand.

Veterans like Jack made my job very easy. They submitted good cartoons, from which I selected the best, and then at the weekly cartoon meeting with the editor (first Tina Brown, then David Remnick), the best of the best would be chosen to go into the magazine. I felt like I was at the controls of a very smoothly functioning machine for creating, selecting, and publishing cartoons. And, frankly, a machine that could pretty much run on automatic pilot with just a little monitoring and tweaking to keep it on course.

Which, at the time, I thought was a good thing because I had a whole other job—actually two whole other jobs: president of the Cartoon Bank and *New Yorker* cartoonist—to occupy and preoccupy me. So every afternoon when my cartoon-editing duties at *The New Yorker* were done,

It was both exhilarating and exhausting. But I had no reason to complain. Of course, that didn't stop me. Does it stop anyone?

"Oh, can't complain, but I do."

And even if I had complained, no one would have taken me seriously, because on the face of it, any one of those jobs is a dream job.

In the beginning, I focused most of my energies on the Cartoon Bank. As a start-up business, it could not survive on autopilot. And frankly, at that point, while being cartoon editor of *The New Yorker* was the prestige cartoon job to end all prestige cartoon jobs, my ego was still mostly invested in being president of the Cartoon Bank. It was my baby, and if things went right, it would grow up to be a win-win for everyone. But as cartoonist David Sipress points out, that's never assured.

"You say it's a win-win, but what if you're wrong-wrong and it all goes bad-bad?"

Long story short, it didn't go bad-bad. It ended up being a good-good thing both for *The New Yorker* and for the cartoonists, who got, and get, significant supplementary income from it: in royalty payments when the cartoons are licensed for use in textbooks, newsletters, and PowerPoint presentations for business or are bought as framed prints by individuals.

But by devoting so much energy to the livelihoods of the present generation of cartoonists, I was neglecting future generations. This wonderful plane flying on autopilot needed some actual piloting or it was going to run out of fuel. Unless I shifted my course, all that would be left of the *New Yorker* cartoon tradition would be found in cartoon anthologies.

So, I would have to do what Lee had done and find some new cartoonists. One immediately came to mind, a man whose addition to the staff would be a win-win for everyone. That's right, you got it: David Sipress, whose cartoon I just featured. He had been banging on *The New Yorker*'s Cartoon Department door for a long time but for some reason had never been able to get in. Even though the number of markets for cartoons had dwindled over the decades, there were some left and David had been successful in those. And he had been an early member of the Cartoon Bank, before *The New Yorker* acquired it. With David, all I had to do was open the door, and a fully formed cartoonist came barging through. David has become the go-to guy for what we call our A-issue cartoons—cartoons that will appear in the next issue. And his gift for being topically on target made him our first choice when we launched our web-only Daily Cartoon feature.

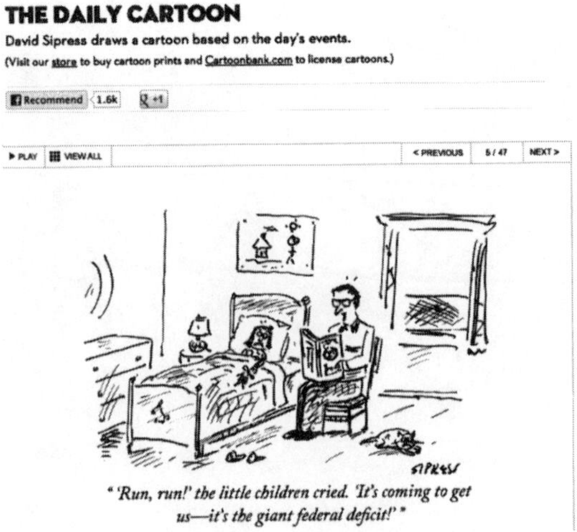
THE DAILY CARTOON
David Sipress draws a cartoon based on the day's events.
(Visit our store to buy cartoon prints and Cartoonbank.com to license cartoons.)
Recommend
1.6k
+1
PLAY
VIEW ALL
< PREVIOUS
5 / 47
NEXT >
SIPRESS
"'Run, run!' the little children cried. 'It's coming to get us—it's the giant federal deficit!'"

Another established talent immediately available was Bill Haefeli, who had done cartoons for the venerable *Punch* magazine, in England. He was also an early member of the Cartoon Bank, so I was familiar with and an admirer of his work. He entered *The New Yorker* with this cartoon, in 1998:

"Teri tells me you're ostensibly straight."

Bill says that when he was growing up, he never thought being gay would be a professional asset, but once homosexuality and the issues surrounding it became an irrefutable part of the cultural landscape, he didn't have to look far afield for material.

"I have two children from a previous sexuality."

"I have two mommies. I know where the apostrophe goes."

And it goes without saying—but I'll say it anyway—that Bill can turn his gimlet eye and pen on the straight world

"Perhaps your performance anxiety wouldn't be so bad if you performed better."

and the rest of the cultural landscape as well.

"I'm cutting articles out of the newspaper while we still can."

A few other established talents came in at about the same time. J. C. Duffy, from the comic-strip world,

"Stella!"

Chris Weyant, from editorial cartooning,

"Susan, this might be just the wine talking, but I think I want to order more wine."

and Harry Bliss, who was already a cover artist for *The New Yorker*.

"Artie, they took my bowl."

In 2002, this group was joined by Drew Dernavich. Drew had a fine arts background in printmaking but preferred to work in humor, drawing political cartoons for a variety of weekly newspapers in Boston. After years of trying out different styles and cartoon formats, he finally settled on a woodcut-like style, but the editors for whom he had previously worked told him, "These are not cartoons." What can I say? Boston weekly editorial cartooning's loss was mine and *The New Yorker*'s gain.

"*Now is the part of the show when we ask the audience to shout out some random numbers.*"

"*The Court will allow the cape but will draw the line at the wind machine.*"

Unfortunately, I soon realized that cherry-picking talent wasn't going to be sufficient, because there just weren't enough cherries out there.

The New Yorker was still standing tall, however: a cartoon edifice among the rubble of former cartoon markets, a beacon to those who dreamed my dream, of cartooning where Addams, Arno, and Thurber had, and now Chast, Ziegler, Cullum, Kaplan, and others did.

To quote Alex Gregory, who has since become one of our stars:

> For the record, I never wanted to become a cartoonist. I still don't. I have only wanted to draw cartoons for *The New Yorker*. For the life of me, I can't remember when I realized I wanted to become a *New Yorker* cartoonist or why, really. I just know that while the other boys my age in New Jersey were stealing mopeds and shooting each other with BB guns in the woods, I spent way too much time in libraries poring over *New Yorker* anthologies and how-to-cartoon books.

But for Alex and others to get a foot in the door, I needed to open the door a bit wider. That's why in 1998 I established Open-Call Tuesdays, where anyone who wanted to show me cartoons could make an appointment to see me. Previously, that privilege had been restricted to established *New Yorker* cartoonists. In fact, it took me a whole year of being published before I was invited to show my cartoons in person.

I thought Open-Call Tuesdays was a great idea, that in and of itself it would bring a bunch of new cartoonists to the magazine. And a lot of fresh-faced aspirants did show up.

But I was still asking them to suck it up, like I had, and take rejection week in and week out. Not only accept it but embrace it. I told them it would make them better cartoonists and better people. Look how much better it made me.

Unhappily, my rejection-to-redemption story did not inspire them; it scared many of them off. They were disappearing into the wilds of advertising, illustration, animation, and sitcom writing, because the other major magazines that previously used cartoons had mostly disappeared, and all I was handing out, besides good wishes, were rejections.

If aspiring cartoonists were not selling here, they were not selling anywhere. This was not a reinforcement schedule that was going to produce persistence. It's as if in baseball the minor leagues had been eliminated and you had to make the New York Yankees right out of high school.

If *New Yorker* cartoons weren't going to become museum pieces, we were going to have to be the minor leagues as well as the majors. We were going to have to break with tradition, in order for the tradition of cartoons in *The New Yorker* to continue. Honestly, I wasn't all that happy about this. Why shouldn't the new generation have the privilege of covering their bathroom walls with rejection slips? It wasn't just that I wanted younger cartoonists to suffer as I had; I understood that you learn more from your failures than your successes. But I realized that if all you ended up having were failures, all you would have learned is how to fail.

So I broke the code of silence and became a real blabbermouth, giving aspiring cartoonists feedback and developing a mini course in cartoon fundamentals and the psychology of humor.

For instance, the punch line comes at the end of the joke, and when it ends, the joke should, too. Like this,

"There you have it, gentlemen—the upside potential is tremendous, but the downside risk is jail."

not this:

"There you have it, gentlemen—the downside risk is jail, but the upside potential is tremendous."

And yes, things are funnier in threes because you need a sequence of at least two to create the right surprise. Without surprise, there is no joke. Surprise requires a setup sequence to work most effectively. Usually what's called a "triplet" is involved, with two items leading to a third, which functions as the punch line.

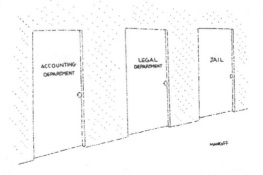

I explained to my quasi students that if I had just a door in an office setting with "Jail" on it, there would not be the tension that can be released by the "punch."

This "triplet" structure applied to captions, as well.

"The amnio's fine, the sex is male, and the name is Wade."

Over time, the mini course became somewhat major, dealing with all the technicalities of the craft as applied to both ideas and graphics.

But if I had to wait for new cartoonists to assimilate all the rules and produce perfect cartoons before they could get into the magazine, I would be waiting a very long time. And time wasn't on my side.

In the past, "close" had always meant "close but no cigar"—in other words, not quite good enough to win the prize of getting into *The New Yorker*. However, now close could be good enough to get published. The truth is, we (I couldn't have done this without David Remnick's full support) were cutting new cartoonists some slack, doing some affirmative action, giving them some reinforcements to get them hooked on cartooning the way I had been.

Two early examples of this were Matt Diffee and Alex Gregory. Matt came to my attention in 1998 because he had won an early version of the cartoon caption contest that had been sponsored by *The New Yorker*'s business department. Raised as a religious fundamentalist, Matt had graduated from Bob Jones University. However, he'd majored not in fundamentalism but art. He'd also headed a comedy team called the Leaping Pickles, which, he wryly remarks, put the "fun" in fundamentalism. So Matt could draw and he was funny—good qualities in a potential cartoonist.

I met with Matt and encouraged him to start submitting. Unfortunately, his submissions indicated that his potential was still mostly unrealized. But, to give Matt a taste of what success would be like, at the weekly cartoon meeting I asked David Remnick to buy this cartoon. Looking back, Matt would probably agree that it would not make his highlight reel.

Still, as I've said, the journey of a thousand cartoons begins with a single one, and this was Matt's. He didn't sell another drawing for eight months, but that first taste, plus the moral support, was enough to keep him going. And when he finally got published again, the improvement was obvious, both in the idea, which is not just a twist on a common cartoon cliché, and in the drawing, which also departs from traditional cartoon conventions by creating a fantasy scenario,

depicted through a very realistic drawing style, a style that demonstrates that Matt's fine arts training was not wasted.

Over the years, Matt has perfected this approach. Here are four of my favorite cartoons of his:

"From the violent nature of the multiple stab wounds, I'd say the victim was probably a consultant."

"Before we begin this family meeting, how about we go around and say our names and a little something about ourselves."

The Vesparados

By the way, that one of Che wearing a Bart Simpson T-shirt has become one of the best-selling cartoons of all time at the Cartoon Bank. I'm sure that years from now, when people complain that *New Yorker* cartoons are not as good as they used to be, this is one of the ones they will be referring to.

But this one probably won't:

Don't get me wrong: it's a funny cartoon and the first one we published from Alex Gregory, who, when all is said and done and drawn, will go down as a great *New Yorker* cartoonist. It's just that this first one wasn't that great. We published it because we saw the potential.

Alex definitely had the comedy chops. He didn't need any tutoring in "triplets" or anything else. At the time we published that cartoon, he was writing for *The Larry Sanders Show*. You don't get that kind of gig without those chops. And he has gone on to more comedy success in TV and movies. Chops indeed.

"Luckily, none of the people inside appear to be celebrities."

But as much as I liked his jokes, I felt that his jokes deserved better drawing.

We talked about it, and he told me his biggest hurdle was his neurotic perfectionism. Mistakes—a smudge, an errant line—made him apoplectic. They filled the drawing process with fear and dread. The clouds parted for Alex when he discovered the Wacom tablet and Adobe Illustrator.

An electronic paintbrush and an eraser proved to be the perfect match for Alex's neurotic perfectionism. He could screw up all he wanted to and in the end not screw up at all. Using this tool, his technique rapidly evolved from blah to a brilliant modernistic drawing style that is as incisive as his wit.

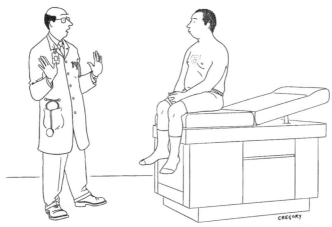

"Whoa—way too much information!"

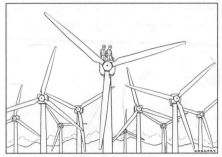

"Try blowing on it."

"I started my vegetarianism for health reasons, then it became a moral choice, and now it's just to annoy people."

"I need someone well versed in the art of torture—do you know PowerPoint?"

Like Alex Gregory, *New Yorker* cartoonist-to-be Paul Noth had good comedy credentials. A regular guest writer for *Late Night with Conan O'Brien*, he'd created the cartoon-animation segment "Pale Force," which featured Conan and stand-up comedian Jim Gaffigan.

And as we'd done with Matt and Alex, we gave Paul a break on this, his first, cumbersomely drawn cartoon for *The New Yorker*, to encourage him:

"How do you respond to critics who claim you're just trying to scare people?"

This one, too:

"Didn't I tell you Tom was fun?"

And a few others. Then I threw the book at him, the book being *The Complete Cartoons of The New Yorker*. I told him to make it his bible and study the techniques of the masters. He would be the first to say that his cartooning is a work in progress, but meanwhile, he's progressing very nicely.

"I was against Russo-Disneyland from the start."

"He's all right. I just wish he were a little more pro-Israel."

With this general approach of encouragement, nudging, noodging, coaching, and cajoling, plus a lucky break, I was able to slowly build a new crew to go along with the old crew, and the recent recruits now produce over half the cartoons that appear in the magazine.

The lucky break was Zach Kanin. Every two or three years I get a new cartoon assistant, a young man or woman who filters all the cartoon submissions for me, as well as the caption contest entries, and also traffics the cartoons through the submission, acceptance, and publication process.

There is a lot of strictly clerical stuff involved, but I need more than a clerk—or at the very least, a clerk with a very good sense of humor.

In 2004, when my previous assistant's term was up, David Remnick made the brilliant suggestion that I call *The Harvard Lampoon* to see if anyone was interested. When I called, it was Zach who picked up the phone, and he was interested. Zach was president of the *Lampoon*, following in the footsteps of the likes of Conan O'Brien. That was a little hard for Zach, because he's short and Conan is tall, so the footstep following required some major leaping as well.

Kanin

Still, as you can see, Zach has a talent that Conan does not: cartooning. In the fourth grade he submitted a cartoon to the then editor, Tina Brown, in which a hunter standing over a dead Donald Duck lying in a pool of blood yells to another hunter, "Hey, Tom, you might want to take a look at this one." And when asked, for his fifth-grade yearbook, what he wanted to be doing in the year 2010, Zach said he hoped to be a famous cartoonist who has a monkey bodyguard trained in jujitsu.

How naïve that youngster was. Firstly, all monkey bodyguards are trained in tae kwon do, and secondly, even the slightest bit of fame spoils a cartoonist rotten. Look what it did to me.

I hired Zach and by becoming my assistant he, in effect, went to *New Yorker* Cartoon College. Part of that entailed listening to me babble incessantly about my half-baked, three-quarters baked, and fully baked theories of humor, but much more important for him was reviewing the thousand cartoons that come in to the magazine every week. He saw the work ethic of *New Yorker* cartoonists firsthand and how high they set the bar for themselves. He immediately bought into the process and started to submit his own batches of cartoons. And he kept at it, week after week. Just like those of Matt and Alex and Paul Noth before him, they showed enough potential to permit a bit of temporary bar lowering to get his first cartoon into the magazine, with this topical mash-up from October 2005:

THE 40-YEAR-OLD VIRGIN OLIVE OIL

It wasn't until five months later that this one appeared:

"Everybody else's problems are better than mine."

Funny, in a *New Yorker* cartoon–ish sort of way. Not that there's anything wrong with that, I, of all people, should add, but my hope for Zach was that he would bring something new to the form, develop his own comedic voice and a consistent drawing style to go with it. By 2007, those two elements had gelled.

"Alright, now see what happens when you turn the faucet off."

"Who let the dining-room set into the liquor cabinet again?"

In the following four years we published, respectively, ten, twenty, thirty-three, and forty-five cartoons by Zach, and he now appears in the magazine almost every week. Zach long ago passed the point where he needs the bar lowered to get into the magazine, and he continues to push himself to go not merely over it, but way over.

Kanin

"Over, damn you, over!"

When Zach's time as assistant was over (I usually boot them out after a couple of years, because at that point reviewing all the caption contest entries has put them on the cusp of madness), I doubled down on my luck and reached out to *The Harvard Lampoon* again. And in came Farley Katz, Zach's fellow cartoon colleague at the *Lampoon*. He also got the cartoon college treatment. He remembers that the most significant advice I gave him was on a Post-it note on one of his cartoon batches. It read, "Tone it down—your characters all look like they're on crack." He did and has been selling cartoons to us ever since. They all still sort of look like they're on crack,

"Today, class, I'm proud to announce my tenure."

even this fractalized giraffe:

But in a good way.

Well, I could go on about each wonderful new cartoonist, and how wonderful I was to make them so wonderful (believe me, I could), but at this point I'll let the new crew speak for themselves in the most appropriate way possible, with some of their best cartoons. Normally, by the power vested in me as cartoon editor, I would pick these, but at this point, I think the master might learn more from the students than the other way around.

ALEX GREGORY

"Let's go, Barney—I guess _some_ people just don't like dogs."

"Tell me the truth—have I ever made tea come out of your nose?"

ON BOB'S DESK

KIM WARP

ARIEL MOLVIG

MOLVIG

BEN SCHWARTZ

"Et tu, Killbot 9000?"

BILL HAEFELI

"If it's not safe to go in the water and it's not safe
to go in the sun, why did you bring me here?"

BOB ECKSTEIN

CAROLITA JOHNSON

"Whoa! That's a little clingy."

"For the love of God, is there a doctor in the house?"

CHRIS WEYANT

"Due to an incident at the Bergen Street station, everything has changed and nothing will ever be the same."

DAVID SIPRESS

DREW DERNAVICH

CARIBBEAN AIRPORT SECURITY

ED STEED

"Well, the sooner we get all this lead turned into gold, the sooner we can go home."

"Is it shoot a cold, stab a fever?"

EMILY FLAKE

FARLEY KATZ

HARRY BLISS

"Slow down, I want to take a peek in Barneys!"

J.C. DUFFY

"Seriously, who is it?"

JOE DATOR

*"Hang on, I think I know what
we're doing wrong."*

KAAMRAN HAFEEZ

"I'll be passing my tape measure over your buttocks, then coming up the inside of your leg. Is that O.K.?"

AMY HWANG

LIAM WALSH

"It keeps me from looking at my phone every two seconds."

FENDI BAG LADY

NEED MATCHING SHOES PLEASE HELP

MARISA ACOCELLA MARCHETTO

MATT DIFFEE

FACE PAINTING
FIVE BUCKS

MICHAEL SHAW

"Thou shalt not create graven images, Ira. Thou shalt not take the Lord's name in vain. Still looking at you, Ira. Thou shalt keep holy the Sabbath. You getting this, Ira?"

PAUL NOTH

"Escher! Get your ass up here."

ROBERT LEIGHTON

TOM TORO

"Yes, the planet got destroyed. But for a beautiful moment in time we created a lot of value for shareholders."

"You wanted to role-play—I can't help it if a doctor would be medically obligated to say something about your weight."

ZACH KANIN

PAT BYRNES

"Put the punster in with the mime."

"Any clues?"

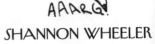

SHANNON WHEELER

The fact is that this new generation is showing what it means to be true to the *New Yorker* cartoon tradition while also changing it, and sometimes even mangling it, but still managing to keep the DNA of the *New Yorker* cartoon alive and endlessly replicating even as it evolves. When will all of this stop? How about never? Never is good for me.

ACKNOWLEDGMENTS

Books don't get published without publishers, and I've been very lucky to have one of the best, Henry Holt and Company. Unfortunately, I never got to meet Mr. Holt, because he passed away in 1926, but, fortunately, a meeting with the successor of his successors, Steve Rubin (and company), resulted in the thumbs-up for this book.

So, many thanks to Steve, his thumb, and the company he keeps, especially editor in chief Gillian Blake, my own personal editor, who deserves a gillion thanks for poring over the cascade of words and images I submitted, helping to turn an inchoate mess into the choate one you're holding.

Well, that's all for the thanks part of this—now on to the deep gratitude section. *The New Yorker* has been my professional home for over half my life. Through it, I've met my best friends, done my best work as a cartoonist, and had the privilege of working with the top cartoonists and editors.

First and foremost among the latter is David Remnick, who is able, even with all his very serious responsibilities, to understand and support the very semi-serious business of cartooning. And who, even when we don't see eye to eye on a cartoon (he's a galling inch and a quarter taller) will sometimes graciously accede to seeing things my way.

Hey, it doesn't get much better than that—except, hey, it does, because of my third, best, and, honest to God, last wife, Cory Scott Whittier. Professional homes are all well and good, and there's none better than *The New Yorker*, but a real home, to paraphrase Robert Frost, is the place where when you go there, they have to let you in. And Cory always has, even if sometimes requiring ID.

Really, she doesn't need it. She knows me better than anyone else and, despite that, has always stood by me, out of loyalty and love, but also to be close enough to whack me upside my head, in order to knock sense into it and foolishness out. My "life in cartoons" would just be a joke without her.

ILLUSTRATION CREDITS

4. © Paul Noth/*The New Yorker* Collection/2012
5. top © Sam Gross/*The New Yorker* Collection/2008
5. bottom © Corey Pandolph/*The New Yorker* Collection/2012
6. © Victoria Roberts/*The New Yorker* Collection/2000
9. © Robert Mankoff/*The New Yorker* Collection/1999
12. © Robert Mankoff/*The New Yorker* Collection/1990
13. © Robert Mankoff/*The New Yorker* Collection/1988
14. © Leonard Dove/*The New Yorker* Collection/1945
15. top © Garrett Price/*The New Yorker* Collection/1956
15. bottom © Warren Miller/*The New Yorker* Collection/1979
17. © Frank Modell/*The New Yorker* Collection/1962
18. top © Arnie Levin/*The New Yorker* Collection/1976
18. bottom © Matthew Diffee/*The New Yorker* Collection/2004
20. © Victoria Roberts/*The New Yorker* Collection/2001
21. © David Sipress/*The New Yorker* Collection/2000
27. top © Robert Mankoff/*The New Yorker* Collection/1997
27. bottom © Robert Mankoff/*The New Yorker* Collection/1990
28. top © Robert Mankoff/*The New Yorker* Collection/1991
28. bottom © Robert Mankoff/*The New Yorker* Collection/2009
29. top © Robert Mankoff/*The New Yorker* Collection/2002
29. bottom © Robert Mankoff/*The New Yorker* Collection/2005
35. © J. B. Handelsman/*The New Yorker* Collection/1985
37. top © Reprinted with the permission of Syd Hoff Trust
37. bottom © Robert Mankoff/ Unpublished
38. © Robert Mankoff/ Unpublished
41. © Robert Mankoff/ Unpublished
43. © Robert Mankoff/ *The Saturday Review of Literature*, 1975
44. © Robert Mankoff/ *National Lampoon*, 1978
47. top © The Saul Steinberg Foundation/Artists Rights Society (ARS), New York, originally published in *The New Yorker*, 1961, Untitled, Ink on paper
47. bottom © Peter Arno/*The New Yorker* Collection/1940
48. top © James Thurber/*The New Yorker* Collection/1937
48. bottom John Leech, published in *Punch* Magazine, 1843
49. Bernard Partridge, published in *Punch* Magazine, 1899
50. top Charles Frederick Peters, *Life* Magazine/1915
50. bottom Reginald Bathurst Birch, *Life* Magazine/1918
51. top © Gilbert Wilkinson/*The New Yorker* Collection/1925
51. bottom © Edward Graham/*The New Yorker* Collection/1927
52. © Carl Rose/*The New Yorker* Collection/1928
53. top © Robert Mankoff/*The New Yorker* Collection/2012
53. bottom © James Thurber/*The New Yorker* Collection/1932
54. © George Price/*The New Yorker* Collection/1936
55. © Peter Arno/*The New Yorker* Collection/1941
58. top © James Stevenson/*The New Yorker* Collection/1991
58. bottom © George Booth/*The New Yorker* Collection/1975
59. top © James Stevenson/*The New Yorker* Collection/1976
59. bottom © James Thurber/*The New Yorker* Collection/1932
60. top © J. B. Handelsman/*The New Yorker* Collection/1968
60. bottom © Dana Fradon/*The New Yorker* Collection/1976
61. top © William Steig/*The New Yorker* Collection/1971
61. bottom © The Saul Steinberg Foundation/Artists Rights Society (ARS), New York, originally published in *The New Yorker*, 1958
62. top © The Saul Steinberg Foundation/Artists Rights Society (ARS), New York, originally published in *The New Yorker*, 1962
62. bottom © The Saul Steinberg Foundation/Artists Rights Society

(ARS), New York, originally published in *The New Yorker*, 1960.
63. top © Robert Mankoff/*The Saturday Review of Literature*, 1976
63. bottom © Robert Mankoff/*Elementary: The Cartoonist Did It*, Avon Books, 1980
64. top © James Thurber/*The New Yorker* Collection/1933
64. bottom © James Thurber/*The New Yorker* Collection/1935
65. top © Robert Mankoff/*Urban Bumpkins*, St. Martin's Press, 1984
65. bottom © Robert Mankoff/*Urban Bumpkins*, St. Martin's Press, 1984
66. top © Robert Mankoff/1984
66. bottom © Robert Mankoff/*The New Yorker* Collection/1979
67. top © Robert Mankoff/*The New Yorker* Collection/1981
67. bottom © George Price/*The New Yorker* Collection/1939
68. © Charles Saxon/*The New Yorker* Collection/1969
69. top © James Thurber/*The New Yorker* Collection/1932
69. bottom © James Thurber/*The New Yorker* Collection/1933
71. © Robert Mankoff/*The Saturday Review of Literature*, 1975
72. top © Robert Mankoff/*The Saturday Review of Literature*, 1975
72. bottom © Robert Mankoff/ Unpublished
74. © Robert Mankoff/ Unpublished
75. © Robert Mankoff/*The Saturday Review of Literature*, 1977
76. © Robert Mankoff/ Unpublished
77. top © Robert Mankoff/*Elementary: The Cartoonist Did It*, Avon Books, 1980
77. bottom © Robert Mankoff/*Urban Bumpkins*, St. Martin's Press, 1984
78. top © Robert Mankoff/ Unpublished
78. bottom © Robert Mankoff/*Elementary: The Cartoonist Did It*, Avon Books, 1980
79. top © Robert Mankoff/*Elementary: The Cartoonist Did It*, Avon Books, 1980
79. bottom © Robert Mankoff/*Elementary: The Cartoonist Did It*, Avon Books, 1980
80. top © Robert Mankoff/ Unpublished
80. middle © Robert Mankoff/ Unpublished
80. bottom © Robert Mankoff/ Unpublished
81. top © Mischa Richter/*The New Yorker* Collection/1972
81. bottom © Robert Mankoff/*The Naked Cartoonist*, Blackdog and Leventhal, 2002
82. top © Robert Mankoff/*The Naked Cartoonist*, Blackdog and Leventhal, 2002
82. bottom © Robert Mankoff/*Urban Bumpkins*, St. Martin's Press, 1984
83. top © Robert Mankoff/*Urban Bumpkins*, St. Martin's Press, 1984
83. bottom © Robert Mankoff/Unpublished
84. top © Robert Mankoff/Unpublished version of first cartoon in *The New Yorker*
84. bottom © Robert Mankoff/*The New Yorker* Collection/1977
89. © Mick Stevens/*The New Yorker* Collection/1979
91. © Jack Ziegler/*The New Yorker* Collection/1974
92. top © Michael Maslin/Unpublished
92. bottom © Whitney Darrow, Jr./*The New Yorker* Collection/1977
93. © Michael Maslin/*The New Yorker* Collection/1978

94. © Roz Chast/*The New Yorker* Collection/1978
96. © Helen E. Hokinson/*The New Yorker* Collection/1938
97. top © Helen E. Hokinson/*The New Yorker* Collection/1946
97. bottom © George Price/*The New Yorker* Collection/1978
98. © Michael Crawford/*The New Yorker* Collection/1983
99. top © Danny Shanahan/*The New Yorker* Collection/1989
99. bottom © Bruce Eric Kaplan/*The New Yorker* Collection/1994
100. top © Robert Mankoff/*The New Yorker* Collection/1977
100. bottom © Robert Mankoff/*The New Yorker* Collection/1977
101. © Robert Mankoff/*The New Yorker* Collection/1977
102. © Robert Mankoff/*The New Yorker* Collection/1979
103. © Robert Mankoff/*The New Yorker* Collection/1978
104. top © Robert Mankoff/*The New Yorker* Collection/1980
104. bottom © Robert Mankoff/*The New Yorker* Collection/1980
105. top © Robert Mankoff/*The New Yorker* Collection/1980
105. bottom © Robert Mankoff/*The New Yorker* Collection/1980
106. © Robert Mankoff/*The New Yorker* Collection/1979
107. © Jack Ziegler/Unpublished
108. top © Charles Saxon/*The New Yorker* Collection/1983
108. bottom © Robert Mankoff/*The New Yorker* Collection/1980
109. top © Robert Mankoff/*The New Yorker* Collection/1980
109. bottom © Robert Mankoff/*The New Yorker* Collection/1983
110. top © Robert Mankoff/*The New Yorker* Collection/1982
110. bottom © Robert Mankoff/*The New Yorker* Collection/1980
111. top © Robert Mankoff/*The New Yorker* Collection/1983
111. bottom © Robert Mankoff/*The New Yorker* Collection/1983
112. © Robert Mankoff/*The New Yorker* Collection/1985
115. © William Hamilton/*The New Yorker* Collection/1979
116. top © Robert Mankoff/*The New Yorker* Collection/1989
116. bottom © Robert Mankoff/*The New Yorker* Collection/1988
117. top © Robert Mankoff/*The New Yorker* Collection/1986
117. bottom © Robert Mankoff/*Call Your Office*, Topper Books, 1986
118. top © Robert Mankoff/*Call Your Office*, Topper Books, 1986
118. bottom © Robert Mankoff/*The New Yorker* Collection/1997
119. top © Robert Mankoff/*The New Yorker* Collection/1991
119. bottom © Robert Mankoff/*The New Yorker* Collection/1992
120. © Robert Mankoff/*The New Yorker* Collection/1999
121. top © Robert Mankoff/*The New Yorker* Collection/1992
121. bottom © Robert Mankoff/*The New Yorker* Collection/1991
122. © Robert Mankoff/*The New Yorker* Collection/1990
123. © Mischa Richter/*The New Yorker* Collection/1958
124. © Robert Mankoff/*The New Yorker* Collection/1979
125. top © Robert Mankoff/*The Saturday Review of Literature*, 1982
125. bottom © Robert Mankoff/*The New Yorker* Collection/1985
127. © Robert Mankoff/*The New Yorker* Collection/2001
128. top © Sam Gross, published *National Lampoon*, 1975
128. bottom © Sam Gross, published *National Lampoon*, 1970
131. © Robert Mankoff/*The New Yorker* Collection/1989
133. © Robert Mankoff/*The New Yorker* Collection/1993
138. © Mike Twohy/*The New Yorker* Collection/1994
140. © Michael Maslin/*The New Yorker* Collection/1997
142. top © Lee Lorenz/*The New Yorker* Collection/1993
142. middle © Mike Twohy/*The New Yorker* Collection/1997
142. bottom © Bernard Schoenbaum/*The New Yorker* Collection/1998
143. © Danny Shanahan/*The New Yorker* Collection/1998
144. top © Robert Mankoff/*The New Yorker* Collection/1994
144. bottom © William Hamilton/*The New Yorker* Collection/1998
145. © Robert Weber/*The New Yorker* Collection/1998
147. © Leo Cullum/*The New Yorker* Collection/1997
148. top © Sam Gross/*The New Yorker* Collection/1998
148. middle © J. B. Handelsman/*The New Yorker* Collection/1997
148. bottom © Tom Cheney/*The New Yorker* Collection/1997

149. © Bruce Eric Kaplan/*The New Yorker* Collection/1998
153. top © Robert Mankoff/*The New Yorker* Collection/2000
153. bottom © Robert Mankoff/*The New Yorker* Collection/1998
154. © Robert Mankoff/*The New Yorker* Collection/1979
156. top © Jack Ziegler/*The New Yorker* Collection/2001
156. bottom © Leo Cullum/*The New Yorker* Collection/1998
157. top © Michael Maslin/*The New Yorker* Collection/2000
157. bottom © Jack Ziegler/*The New Yorker* Collection/1990
158. © Pat Byrnes/*The New Yorker* Collection/2000
159. © Danny Shanahan/*The New Yorker* Collection/2005
160. © Roz Chast/*The New Yorker* Collection/1980
161c. © Harry Bliss/*The New Yorker* Collection/2003
161b. © Leo Cullum/*The New Yorker* Collection/2002
161a. © David Sipress/*The New Yorker* Collection/2003
161. diagram © Mary Ann Rishel/*Writing Humor*, Wayne State University: 2002.
161. bottom © Alex Gregory/*The New Yorker* Collection/2001
166. © Jack Ziegler/*The New Yorker* Collection/1995
168. © Mick Stevens/*The New Yorker* Collection/2012
169. © Jack Ziegler/*The New Yorker* Collection/2012
171. © Matthew Diffee/*The New Yorker* Collection/2012
175. top © Roz Chast/*The New Yorker* Collection/1983
175. bottom © Roz Chast/*The New Yorker* Collection/1993
177. top © David Sipress/*The New Yorker* Collection/2008
177. bottom © David Sipress/*The New Yorker* Collection/2010
178. top © David Sipress/*The New Yorker* Collection/2000
178. bottom © David Sipress/*The New Yorker* Collection/2011
179. © Jack Ziegler/*The New Yorker* Collection/2006
184. top © Liam Walsh/*The New Yorker* Collection/2011
184. bottom © Liam Walsh/*The New Yorker* Collection/2012
185. top © Liam Walsh/Unpublished
185. bottom © Robert Mankoff/*The New Yorker* Collection/2005
186. © Liam Walsh/*The New Yorker* Collection/2013
187. © Danny Shanahan/*The New Yorker* Collection/2012
188. © Sam Gross/*The New Yorker* Collection/2009
189. top © Mort Gerberg/*The New Yorker* Collection/1998
189. bottom © David Sipress/*The New Yorker* Collection/2004
190. top © Ed Fisher/*The New Yorker* Collection/1955
190. middle © Sam Gross/*The New Yorker* Collection/1981
190. bottom © Peter Steiner/*The New Yorker* Collection/1990
191. © Tom Cheney/*The New Yorker* Collection/2005
192. © Edward Frascino/*The New Yorker* Collection/1968
193. top © Robert Mankoff/*The New Yorker* Collection/1993
193. bottom © David Sipress/ Unpublished
194. top left © Warren Miller/*The New Yorker* Collection/1990
194. top right © Henry Martin/*The New Yorker* Collection/1989
194. bottom © Al Ross/*The New Yorker* Collection/1991
195. top © Liam Walsh
195. bottom © Paul Noth/*The New Yorker* Collection/2013
196. top © Michael Crawford/ Unpublished
196. bottom © William Haefeli/*The New Yorker* Collection/2009
197. top © Mick Stevens/Unpublished
197. bottom © Joe Dator/*The New Yorker* Collection/2013
198. top © Roz Chast/*The New Yorker* Collection/2008
198. bottom © Jack Ziegler/*The New Yorker* Collection/2002
199. top © Drew Dernavich/*The New Yorker* Collection/2008
199. bottom © Robert Mankoff/*The New Yorker* Collection/1995
200. © Farley Katz/*The New Yorker* Collection/2012
201. top © Paul Karasik/*The New Yorker* Collection/2013
201. bottom © Edward Koren/*The New Yorker* Collection/2013
202. © Sidney Harris/*The New Yorker* Collection/2012
203. © Bob Eckstein/*The New Yorker* Collection/2012

204. top © Marisa Acocella Marchetto/*The New Yorker* Collection/1998
204. bottom © Michael Maslin/*The New Yorker* Collection/2013
205. © Leo Cullum/*The New Yorker* Collection/2001
209. © Robert Mankoff/ Unpublished
211. top © Jack Ziegler/*The New Yorker* Collection/1996
211. bottom © Pat Byrnes/*The New Yorker* Collection/1999
212. © Barbara Smaller/*The New Yorker* Collection/2012
213. top © Christopher Weyant/*The New Yorker* Collection/2012
213. bottom © J. C. Duffy, published in *The Rejection Collection*, 2010
214. © David Sipress/*The New Yorker* Collection/2006
215. top © John Kane/*The New Yorker* Collection/2004
215. bottom © Robert Mankoff/*The New Yorker* Collection/2007
216. top © Mick Stevens/*The New Yorker* Collection/2001
216. bottom © Alex Gregory/*The New Yorker* Collection/2006
217. top © Bruce Eric Kaplan/*The New Yorker* Collection/2011
217. bottom © William Haefeli/*The New Yorker* Collection/2010
218. © Bruce Eric Kaplan/*The New Yorker* Collection/2007
219. © Corey Pandolph/*The New Yorker* Collection/2012
220. top © Robert Mankoff/*The New Yorker* Collection/1996
220. bottom © Jack Ziegler/*The New Yorker* Collection/1998
221. © Drew Dernavich/*The New Yorker* Collection/2005
225. © Jack Ziegler/*The New Yorker* Collection/2000
226. © Mike Twohy/*The New Yorker* Collection/2005
228. © Frank Cotham/*The New Yorker* Collection/2006
234. © Frank Cotham/*The New Yorker* Collection/2012
236. © Tom Cheney/*The New Yorker* Collection/2011
237. © Jack Ziegler/*The New Yorker* Collection/2008
238. © Danny Shanahan/*The New Yorker* Collection/2006
244. © Whitney Darrow, Jr./*The New Yorker* Collection/1967
245. © Peter Steiner/*The New Yorker* Collection/1993
247. top © Robert Mankoff/*The New Yorker* Collection/2003
247. bottom © David Sipress/*The New Yorker* Collection/2003
248. © David Sipress/ Daily cartoon for newyorker.com
249. top © William Haefeli/*The New Yorker* Collection/1998
249. bottom © William Haefeli/*The New Yorker* Collection/2002
250. top © William Haefeli/*The New Yorker* Collection/2004
250. bottom © William Haefeli/*The New Yorker* Collection/2011
251. top © William Haefeli/*The New Yorker* Collection/2009
251. bottom © J. C. Duffy/*The New Yorker* Collection/2003
252. top © Christopher Weyant/*The New Yorker* Collection/2003
252. bottom © Harry Bliss/*The New Yorker* Collection/2007
253. top © Drew Dernavich/*The New Yorker* Collection/2008
253. bottom © Drew Dernavich/*The New Yorker* Collection/2010
256. top © Robert Mankoff/*The New Yorker* Collection/1985
256. bottom © Robert Mankoff/*The New Yorker* Collection/1985
257. © Robert Mankoff/*The New Yorker* Collection/1993
258. top © Matthew Diffee/*The New Yorker* Collection/1999
258. bottom © Matthew Diffee/*The New Yorker* Collection/1999
259. top left © Matthew Diffee/*The New Yorker* Collection/2001
259. top right © Matthew Diffee/*The New Yorker* Collection/2002

259. bottom left © Matthew Diffee/*The New Yorker* Collection/2006
259. bottom right © Matthew Diffee/*The New Yorker* Collection/2004
260. top © Alex Gregory/*The New Yorker* Collection/1999
260. bottom © Alex Gregory/*The New Yorker* Collection/1999
261. © Alex Gregory/*The New Yorker* Collection/2002
262. top © Alex Gregory/*The New Yorker* Collection/2003
262. middle © Alex Gregory/*The New Yorker* Collection/2003
262. bottom © Alex Gregory/*The New Yorker* Collection/2006
263. top © Paul Noth/Unpublished
263. bottom © Paul Noth/*The New Yorker* Collection/2004
264. top © Paul Noth/*The New Yorker* Collection/2005
264. bottom © Paul Noth/*The New Yorker* Collection/2010
265. top © Paul Noth/*The New Yorker* Collection/2012
265. bottom © Paul Noth/*The New Yorker* Collection/2012
266. © Zachary Kanin/Unpublished
267. top © Zachary Kanin/*The New Yorker* Collection/2005
267. bottom © Zachary Kanin/*The New Yorker* Collection/2006
268. top © Zachary Kanin/*The New Yorker* Collection/2007
268. bottom © Zachary Kanin/*The New Yorker* Collection/2007
269. top © Zachary Kanin/*The New Yorker* Collection/2011
269. bottom © Farley Katz/*The New Yorker* Collection/2009
270. © Farley Katz/*The New Yorker* Collection/2008
271. top © Alex Gregory/*The New Yorker* Collection/2004
271. bottom © Kim Warp/*The New Yorker* Collection/2011
272. top © Ariel Molvig/*The New Yorker* Collection/2008
272. bottom © Benjamin Schwartz/*The New Yorker* Collection/2013
273. top © William Haefeli/*The New Yorker* Collection/2000
273. bottom © Bob Eckstein/*The New Yorker* Collection/2011
274. top © Carolita Johnson/*The New Yorker* Collection/2010
274. bottom © Christopher Weyant/*The New Yorker* Collection/2006
275. top © David Sipress/*The New Yorker* Collection/2011
275. bottom © Drew Dernavich/*The New Yorker* Collection/2009
276. top © Edward Steed/ Unpublished
276. bottom © Emily Flake/*The New Yorker* Collection/2011
277. top © Farley Katz/*The New Yorker* Collection/2012
277. bottom © Harry Bliss/*The New Yorker* Collection/2012
278. top © J. C. Duffy/*The New Yorker* Collection/2011
278. bottom © Joe Dator/*The New Yorker* Collection/2010
279. top © Kaamran Hafeez/*The New Yorker* Collection/2011
279. bottom © Amy Hwang/*The New Yorker* Collection/2012
280. top © Liam Walsh/*The New Yorker* Collection/2013
280. bottom © Marisa Acocella Marchetto/*The New Yorker* Collection/1999
281. top © Matthew Diffee/*The New Yorker* Collection/2003
281. bottom © Michael Shaw/*The New Yorker* Collection/2006
282. top © Paul Noth/*The New Yorker* Collection/2011
282. bottom © Robert Leighton/*The New Yorker* Collection/2013
283. top © Tom Toro/*The New Yorker* Collection/2012
283. bottom © Zachary Kanin/*The New Yorker* Collection/2010
284. top © Pat Byrnes/*The New Yorker* Collection/2004
284. bottom © Shannon Wheeler/*The New Yorker* Collection/2012